Ralf Laue

Efficient and Flexible Cryptographic Co-Processor Architecture

Ralf Laue

Efficient and Flexible Cryptographic Co-Processor Architecture

Focussing on Server Application

Südwestdeutscher Verlag für Hochschulschriften

Impressum/Imprint (nur für Deutschland/ only for Germany)
Bibliografische Information der Deutschen Nationalbibliothek: Die Deutsche Nationalbibliothek verzeichnet diese Publikation in der Deutschen Nationalbibliografie; detaillierte bibliografische Daten sind im Internet über http://dnb.d-nb.de abrufbar.
Alle in diesem Buch genannten Marken und Produktnamen unterliegen warenzeichen-, marken- oder patentrechtlichem Schutz bzw. sind Warenzeichen oder eingetragene Warenzeichen der jeweiligen Inhaber. Die Wiedergabe von Marken, Produktnamen, Gebrauchsnamen, Handelsnamen, Warenbezeichnungen u.s.w. in diesem Werk berechtigt auch ohne besondere Kennzeichnung nicht zu der Annahme, dass solche Namen im Sinne der Warenzeichen- und Markenschutzgesetzgebung als frei zu betrachten wären und daher von jedermann benutzt werden dürften.

Verlag: Südwestdeutscher Verlag für Hochschulschriften Aktiengesellschaft & Co. KG
Dudweiler Landstr. 99, 66123 Saarbrücken, Deutschland
Telefon +49 681 37 20 271-1, Telefax +49 681 37 20 271-0, Email: info@svh-verlag.de
Zugl.: Damstadt, TU, Diss., 2008

Herstellung in Deutschland:
Schaltungsdienst Lange o.H.G., Berlin
Books on Demand GmbH, Norderstedt
Reha GmbH, Saarbrücken
Amazon Distribution GmbH, Leipzig
ISBN: 978-3-8381-0287-0

Imprint (only for USA, GB)
Bibliographic information published by the Deutsche Nationalbibliothek: The Deutsche Nationalbibliothek lists this publication in the Deutsche Nationalbibliografie; detailed bibliographic data are available in the Internet at http://dnb.d-nb.de.
Any brand names and product names mentioned in this book are subject to trademark, brand or patent protection and are trademarks or registered trademarks of their respective holders. The use of brand names, product names, common names, trade names, product descriptions etc. even without a particular marking in this works is in no way to be construed to mean that such names may be regarded as unrestricted in respect of trademark and brand protection legislation and could thus be used by anyone.

Publisher:
Südwestdeutscher Verlag für Hochschulschriften Aktiengesellschaft & Co. KG
Dudweiler Landstr. 99, 66123 Saarbrücken, Germany
Phone +49 681 37 20 271-1, Fax +49 681 37 20 271-0, Email: info@svh-verlag.de

Copyright © 2009 by the author and Südwestdeutscher Verlag für Hochschulschriften Aktiengesellschaft & Co. KG and licensors
All rights reserved. Saarbrücken 2009

Printed in the U.S.A.
Printed in the U.K. by (see last page)
ISBN: 978-3-8381-0287-0

Danksagungen

Die vorliegende Arbeit entstand während meiner Tätigkeit als wissenschaftlicher Mitarbeiter am Fachgebiet *Integrierte Schaltungen und Systeme* an der Technischen Universität Darmstadt. Ihr Gelingen in dieser Form wäre ohne unzählige fachliche Diskussionen mit meinen Kollegen und Studenten nicht denkbar. Deshalb möchte ich mich an dieser Stelle bei allen bedanken, die dazu beigetragen haben, diese Zeit produktiv und erfolgreich zu machen.

Zuerst danke ich Prof. Dr. Sorin A. Huss für seine hervorragende Betreuung, seine Offenheit für meine Ideen, viele Anregungen und Diskussionen und seine Unterstützung beim Schreiben wissenschaftlicher Publikationen. Danken möchte ich auch Prof. Dr. Johannes Buchmann für die Übernahme des Ko-Referats und sein Interesse an dieser Arbeit.

Während meines Studiums haben Wolfgang Bossung, Michael Jung und Stephan Klaus mir die Arbeit in diesem interessanten Teilgebiet der Informatik ermöglicht. Danken möchte ich dabei vor allem Stephan Klaus und Michael Jung für die Betreuung meiner Semester- bzw. Diplomarbeit.

Besonderer Dank geht natürlich auch an meine Kollegen Tom Assmuth, Prih Hastono, Stephan Hermanns, Dan Honciuc, Michael Jung, Stephan Klaus, Andreas Kühn, Felix Madlener, Gregor Molter, Tim Sander, Abdul Shoufan, Maria Tiedemann, Song Yuan, Jürgen Weber und Kaiping Zeng für viele Diskussionen, ihre Unterstützung und natürlich auch für viele schöne Gespräche am Rande der Arbeit.

Großer Dank gilt auch den Studenten Oliver Kelm, Gregor Molter, Felix Rieder, Kartik Saxena, Sebastian Schipp, Osman Ugus und Boyan Yurukov, die im Rahmen von Diplomarbeiten, Praktika und als studentische Hilfskräfte wertvolle Beiträge zu dieser Arbeit geleistet haben.

Aufgrund der Ausrichtung der Arbeit auf Kryptographie war auch die fachliche Hilfe von Harald Baier, Martin Döring, Birgit Henhapl, Christoph Ludwig, Raphael Overbeck, Daniel Schepers, Tsuyoshi Takagi, Ulrich Vollmer und Ralf-Philipp Weinmann von unschätzbarem Wert. Diesen danke ich für ihre Zeit und Geduld, zu meinem Verständnis der tieferen mathematischen Zusammenhänge der verschiedenen kryptographischen Verfahren beizutragen.

Mein Dank gilt auch dem *Bundesministerium für Bildung und Forschung* (BMBF) für die Finanzierung des Forschungsprojekts SicAri, in dessen Rahmen diese Arbeit entstand. In diesem Zusammenhang möchte ich auch den Projektleitern Harald Baier und Michael Kreutzer für ihre Unterstützung danken.

Schließlich möchte ich in besonderem Maße meinen Eltern danken, die mir diese Ausbildung erst ermöglichten. Danken möchte ich auch meiner Lebensgefährtin Julia, die mich mich in der schwierigen Endphase dieser Arbeit unterstützt hat.

Contents

1. **Introduction**   1
   1.1. Basic co-processor framework 1
   1.2. Common public key approaches 2
   1.3. Parallelization in cryptography 3
   1.4. Short overview on the proposed architecture 3
   1.5. Remainder of this work 5

2. **Related work**   7
   2.1. RSA/ECC combinations 7
   2.2. Cryptographic HW/SW combinations 8
   2.3. Single-chip solutions 9

3. **Mathematical foundations**   11
   3.1. Algebraic structures 11
      3.1.1. Groups 11
      3.1.2. Fields 12
   3.2. Modular arithmetic 13
      3.2.1. Modular operations 13
      3.2.2. Montgomery multiplication 16
      3.2.3. Chinese Remainder Theorem 18
   3.3. Elliptic curve group 18
      3.3.1. Additive operations in affine coordinates 20
      3.3.2. Additive operations in projective coordinates 20
      3.3.3. Point multiplication 23
   3.4. Pairings 23
      3.4.1. General pairings 23
      3.4.2. Tate pairing 24
      3.4.3. Variant of Tate pairing used in this work 25
      3.4.4. Operations in the extension field 26

4. **Cryptographic aspects**   29
   4.1. Public key cryptography 30
      4.1.1. RSA 31
      4.1.2. Elliptic curve cryptography 35
      4.1.3. Pairing-based cryptography 39
   4.2. Abstraction levels 41

Contents

- 4.3. Parallelization for public key cryptography 42
  - 4.3.1. Parallelization on modular arithmetic level 42
  - 4.3.2. Parallelization on intermediate algebraic structure level 44
  - 4.3.3. Parallelization on cryptographic main operation level 45
  - 4.3.4. Cryptographic scheme and system levels 46
- 4.4. Auxiliary cryptographic functions 46
  - 4.4.1. Advanced Encryption Standard 47
  - 4.4.2. Counter-mode encryption 47
  - 4.4.3. Hash function 48
  - 4.4.4. Cryptographically secure random number generator 49
  - 4.4.5. Message Authentication Code 49
  - 4.4.6. Hash-to-point 50

5. Hardware platform   51
- 5.1. XUP Virtex-II Pro Development System 52
- 5.2. Virtex-II Pro FPGA 52
  - 5.2.1. Basic components 53
  - 5.2.2. Derived SoC architecture 54
- 5.3. Design flow 56

6. Novel flexible and efficient co-processor architecture for server applications   57
- 6.1. Architectural decisions 57
  - 6.1.1. HW/SW co-design 58
  - 6.1.2. HW/SW partitioning 58
  - 6.1.3. Modular arithmetic core 59
  - 6.1.4. Parallelization on higher abstraction levels 61
  - 6.1.5. Resulting co-processor architecture 61
- 6.2. Modular arithmetic core 63
  - 6.2.1. Modular multiplication using short pipelines 64
  - 6.2.2. Parallel memory architecture 65
  - 6.2.3. Remaining modular arithmetic 68
- 6.3. Auxiliary function core 70
- 6.4. Scheme controllers 70
- 6.5. Central core 70

7. Prototype implementation   73
- 7.1. Supported functionality 73
- 7.2. Co-processor architecture 75
- 7.3. Modular arithmetic core 77
  - 7.3.1. Interface of the ModArith core 77
  - 7.3.2. Memory configuration 80
  - 7.3.3. Modular multiplication 82
  - 7.3.4. Remaining modular operations 84
- 7.4. Auxiliary function core 86

	7.4.1. Overview on other realizations	86
	7.4.2. Architecture overview and interface	87
	7.4.3. AES module	90
	7.4.4. Auxiliary unit for the counter-mode encryption	91
	7.4.5. Auxiliary unit for the hash function	92
	7.4.6. Auxiliary unit for the random number generator	93
	7.4.7. Performance	93
7.5.	MicroBlaze soft-cores processors	94
	7.5.1. Driver for the ModArith core	95
	7.5.2. Driver for the AES core	96
	7.5.3. Software structure and interface	96
	7.5.4. Realization details for RSA	99
	7.5.5. Realization details for ECC	100
	7.5.6. Realization details for PBC	104
7.6.	Central core	106
7.7.	Inter-processor communication	106
7.8.	Example: RSA encryption	109

8. Results — 111
8.1. Resource usage — 111
8.2. Complete scheme operations — 112
8.3. Cryptographic main operations — 119
8.4. Comparison with other designs — 120

9. Conclusion — 125

A. Parameter set for Type A curves — 129

B. Timing values exploiting just one scheme controller — 131

Bibliography — 135

Chapter 1.
Introduction

Today's client-server networks become increasingly heterogeneous concerning the specifics of the involved devices and protocols. The amount of different client and server platforms is expanding with the accelerating spread of electronic devices, be they mobile or not.

Unfortunately, the utilized communication channels are not secure from attackers on their own. The electronic transfer makes eavesdropping and insertion or substitution of false data relatively easy. However, for many applications, in particular business transactions, a secure communication channel is absolutely necessary.

To obtain such secure channels, the utilized protocols must incorporate cryptography as a building block. This, however, produces a certain computational overhead, because the cryptographic operations have to be executed before the data is transmitted. This is especially true for the computationally expensive *public key cryptography*, which is often necessary to solve the problem, how to securely exchange the keys, see Chapter 4.

Furthermore, as the networks become increasingly heterogeneous, it is also to be expected that the diversity of the cryptographic approaches grows, too. Thus, a server communicating with different client types, likely, has to support a wide range of cryptographic schemes, too.

1.1. Basic co-processor framework

This work focuses on public key operations on servers. The servers must communicate with multiple client devices virtually at the same time and for each of the clients, they must compute an expensive public key operation, at least at the beginning of the session to negotiate a session key. This key may then be used to secure the communication with *secret key cryptography*, which is computationally less expansive. Thus, a possible scenario would be a bank server, which receives bank transfer orders in a secure fashion from client devices.

The proposed cryptographic co-processor architecture is intended to help the server to shoulder this load. It aims for a realization as *System-on-a-Chip* (SoC) design on an FPGA. The intended application of the proposed architecture in servers results in two main consequences:

1. The server should be able to communicate with different client types. Because the different clients may also utilize different cryptographic approaches, the co-

processor should be flexible regarding the supported cryptographic algorithms. This also includes that it should be relatively easy to incorporate new cryptographic protocols, which also aids long-term security.

2. For servers the most important performance criterion is throughput. Thus, low latency of a single operations is less important than a high amount of executed operations per time. However, the latency should not be noticeable for the user, i.e., it should only be a fraction of a second. Otherwise, the cryptographic operations may become the bottleneck of the communication process.

The design of the co-processor as SoC aids both its security as well as its reusability. The security, on the one hand, benefits from the decreased eavesdropping risk of a single-chip design, where all computations are executed on-chip. Thus, secret information does not have to leave the chip, where it could be read directly from the circuit paths. Furthermore, it makes *side channel attacks*[1] more difficult. This is because the power usage and the electromagnetic emissions of the secret computations are partly blinded by the calculations of other cores, in particular, in the proposed architecture, which features several identical cores in parallel. The reusability, on the other hand, is aided because an SoC design encapsulates all required functions. This simplifies the control tasks for the host server.

1.2. Common public key approaches

The most common public key approach today is *RSA*. It is around for a long time and, therefore, features a high trust in its security. However, RSA is computational expensive and its computational complexity increases exponentially with the security level.

A different variety of public key cryptography is *elliptic curve cryptography* (ECC). Although its mathematical foundations are more complex, it operates on numbers of smaller bit-width. Thus, ECC is computational less expensive than RSA and its complexity increases only linearly with the security level. Therefore, it is to be expected that ECC will substitute RSA in most applications in the future.

A server, which has to communicate with a wide range of – maybe – different clients, should at least support RSA and ECC. Fortunately, both utilize modular arithmetic on the lowest level, thus, it is possible to speed up both with the same dedicated hardware. However, because the algorithms of RSA and ECC are quite different on higher levels, it is beneficial to exploit HW/SW co-design. That way, the time-critical modular calculations may be executed in specialized hardware, while the less time-critical control tasks may be realized in software, which is easier to program and debug.

To highlight the flexibility of the proposed co-processor architecture, this work also includes *pairing-based cryptography* (PBC). This third variety of public key cryptography builds on the same foundations as ECC, but utilizes so called *pairings*, too, see Section 3.4. Therefore, it is possible to realize PBC operations using the hardware and software of a combined RSA/ECC design by just including new software functions.

---

[1]See [32] for an overview on side channel attacks

Note in this context that ECC and PBC are realized over finite fields. For both, it is possible to exploit either prime fields $\mathbb{GF}(p)$ or binary fields $\mathbb{GF}(2^m)$. However, in this work only $\mathbb{GF}(p)$ is considered, because dedicated hardware for $\mathbb{GF}(2^m)$ is not usable for RSA. Furthermore, literature offers designs supporting both fields with so called *unified architectures*, see for example [21, 31].

1.3. Parallelization in cryptography

In recent years the increase in possible cycle frequencies has decelerated. However, *Moore's Law*, which predicts a doubling of the available amount of transistors per area, seems still to be valid. Therefore, nowadays the performance increase does mostly stem from higher parallelization of the calculations. Thus, to benefit from better hardware, cryptographic implementations have to take advantage of these parallel resources by exploiting parallel algorithm variants.

The easiest way for this is to parallelize the most important modular operation, namely, the modular multiplication. However, the calculations for RSA typically need numbers with more than 1000 bits, while computations for ECC operate on numbers with only around 200 bits. Although it is possible to reuse the large multipliers intended for RSA, the operations of ECC do not exploit the full width of these multipliers, which leads to unused resources.

This collides with the design goal of high throughput, because high throughput requires the available resources to work as continuously as possible. Therefore, the degree of parallelization within the modular arithmetic is limited, if throughput is of importance and the architecture must be able to work with a wide range of possible bit-widths.

To compensate for the low degree of parallelization in the modular arithmetic, parallelization is also exploited on higher levels, namely, by parallelizing the modular multipliers in each core for modular arithmetic and by also parallelizing those cores. This is explained in more detail in Chapter 6.

Most previous designs from literature did not include ideas how to handle calculations for RSA and ECC at the same time. Furthermore, this work seems to be the first to suggest the exploitation of parallel executions of complete cryptographic schemes, e.g., ECDSA signature generation or RSAES-OAEP encryption.

Note that above only RSA and ECC were considered. This is because the bit-widths of the realized PBC scheme lies somewhere in between these extremes. Thus, a design evenly accelerating the bit-widths range between RSA and ECC also accelerates the bit-widths required for PBC.

1.4. Short overview on the proposed architecture

Figure 1.1 depicts the proposed architecture consisting of several cores, which communicate with each other. The communication with the host server is executed by the *central core*, which controls the other cores, too. In the prototype implementation this role is

Chapter 1. Introduction

assumed by a PowerPC processor and its functionality is realized only partly, because its program just contains functions to test the functionality and the speed of the other cores.

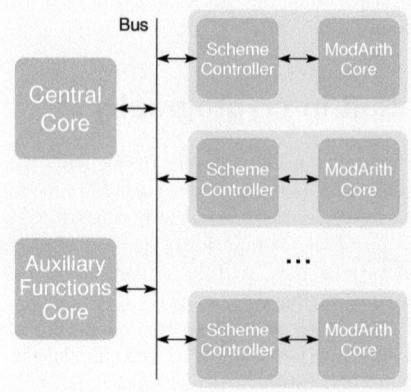

Figure 1.1.: Simplified view of the proposed co-processor architecture

The *ModArith* core is responsible for the calculations in the modular arithmetic. The modular multipliers are pipelined and each ModArith core contains two of these multipliers to accelerate the computations.

The execution of the cryptographic operation is controlled by cores called *scheme controllers*, which each are assigned a single ModArith core to accelerate the modular operations. The scheme controllers are issued commands to execute cryptographic schemes by the central core. In combination with the ModArith cores, the scheme controllers may be parallelized as often as the available resource allow. In the prototype implementation the scheme controllers are realized using MicroBlaze soft-core processors.

Although the modular operations take up the majority of the computational load of a single scheme, some *auxiliary cryptographic functions* are also required. These are symmetric en-/decryption, hash function, and random number generation. To minimize the resource usage of these functions, they are realized in their own core, which is shared between all scheme controllers.

Design history

The idea for the proposed architecture emerged in a vague form in 2005 during the implementation leading to [15]. During the writing of [58], it crystallized in a more concrete form, which was, subsequently, refined and published in [59]. At this point many realization details were still missing. This was changed in a further refinement period, in which the separate parts of the architecture were implemented: Firstly, the core for the auxiliary functions was developed and presented in [61]. Secondly, the interprocessor communication between central core and scheme controllers including code for RSA and ECC was realized, see [79]. Thirdly, the pipelined version of the modular multiplier was created, see [95]. These parts were then integrated, further optimized, and extended by code for PBC leading to the first complete realization, which was presented in [62]. The prototype implementation introduced in this work is mainly the same as in [62]. However, some minor optimizations led to better results.

1.5. Remainder of this work

Chapter 2 presents literature related to this work. However, it is restricted to designs, which exhibit similar aspects to this work. Approaches and algorithms utilized in the proposed architecture or the prototype implementation are referenced at the position in the text they are used. Furthermore, the overview on parallelization in cryptography is deferred to Chapter 4.

Chapter 3 introduces the mathematical foundations necessary for the understanding of this work. These are mainly the definitions of the algebraic structures used for the cryptographic algorithms and how calculations in these structures are executed. The chapter concludes with a basic introduction to pairings, which are required for PBC.

Chapter 4 builds upon the mathematical foundations and details the cryptographic aspects of this work. This centers on Public-Key Cryptography in the three varieties RSA, ECC, and PBC. Furthermore, a classification of these approaches in different abstraction levels is introduced. This is followed by an overview on parallelization possibilities in cryptography. Finally, the auxiliary cryptographic functions necessary for the execution of complete schemes are presented.

Chapter 5 provides a rough overview on the utilized hardware platform, namely, the XUP Virtex-II Pro Development System with the Virtex-II Pro FPGA as central element. The chapter concludes with a short introduction of the design flow used to generate the prototype implementation.

Based on the fundamental information and considerations provided by the previous chapters, Chapter 6 presents the novel flexible and efficient co-processors architecture for server applications. This starts with the constraints, which lead to the architectural decisions. Then, the actual architecture and its individual parts are explained in more detail. This explanation, however, does still abstract from implementation details.

Chapter 7 illustrates the prototype implementation realized to evaluate the validity of the proposed architecture. It starts with the implementation constraints and, subsequently, presents details about all parts of the architecture, i.e., the different cores and how they interact.

Chapter 8 introduces the results of the prototype implementation. This includes the resource usage and the timing figures for different design variants. The chapter closes with a comparison with other realizations from literature.

Chapter 9, finally, concludes this work summarizing the important points. Additionally, some ideas are motivated, which may be considered in future work.

Chapter 2.
Related work

This chapter presents literature introducing approaches and ideas similar to those of this work. In the following, these are divided into *RSA/ECC combinations*, *cryptographic HW/SW combinations*, and *single-chip solutions*, which all three are aspects of this work. Although some of the publications fit into all three categories, most introduce or improve techniques of just one aspect.

This work also utilizes related work beyond these three aspects. This is mainly literature containing cryptographic algorithms, which were utilized in the design of the architecture and for the prototype implementation. Therefore, they are introduced later on in the context of the concrete aspects they were used in. A special case are the proposals for parallelization of algorithms in cryptography. Those are deferred to Section 4.3, because they are presented according to the abstraction level classification, which is given in that chapter, too.

2.1. RSA/ECC combinations

Both RSA and ECC are based on modular arithmetic and it is likely that both approaches will stay with us for the foreseeable future. From the point of view of the modular arithmetic, however, the major difference between both approaches is the huge difference in the utilized bit-widths. For common security levels RSA requires calculations with values of 1000 or more bits, while for ECC the bit-widths range around 200.

Still, because of the similarities between RSA and ECC, many dedicated hardware designs for modular arithmetic over $\mathbb{GF}(p)$ from literature consider them both. In most cases, however, this is done by keeping the designs scalable in terms of the bit-width. This means that the design may be instantiated with any arbitrary bit-width, while its execution time and its resource usage increase only linearly with the bit-width. Examples for such designs may be found in [93, 103, 90, 87, 31, 8].

Thus, the designer may use the architecture to instantiate it as needed, i.e., either for an RSA or an ECC realization. [8] addresses the problem of combined RSA/ECC implementations. Its goal is to extend an already existing RSA implementation by the required ECC functionality: The modular multiplier is reused for ECC and additional modular operation like addition and subtraction are provided in form of a co-processor. Then, it is sufficient to extend the module controlling the modular arithmetic by the algorithms for the EC operations, which build upon the modular operations. The authors also suggest to instantiate and utilize a second modular multiplier allowing to parallelize point addition and doubling. Thus, [8] already allows RSA and ECC on the same hardware. However, the authors do not examine the fact that, while the multiplier is able to operate with small and large bit-widths, large parts of the multiplier will stay unused for operations with smaller bit-widths. Thus, this design does not allow an even and continuous exploitation of all resources.

A solution for this problem is presented in [26]. Its authors propose a hardware module for modular multiplication utilizing pipelining. Similar to previous designs this multiplier is able to operate on values with small or large bit-widths. However, as a specialty the complete multiplier is build up from several smaller modules. Thus, if RSA is to be used, all smaller modules work together like a multiplier of a large bit-width. But for ECC calculations the smaller cores can work in parallel and independently from each other. This way, the amount of unused resources is decreased considerably. However, if RSA and ECC should be possible with different bit-widths, resources are still unused for all computations, which do not operate with a multiple of the bit-width of the smaller cores. Furthermore, a continuous exploitation of the design from [26] also requires a scheduling of the RSA and ECC operations, as during an RSA multiplication no ECC multiplication is possible and vice versa.

2.2. Cryptographic HW/SW combinations

By utilizing HW/SW co-design the data and control flow intensive parts of the cryptographic operations are separated and implemented in hardware and software, respectively. This allows to exploit the respective advantages of hardware and software: The data flow intensive parts, which are time-critical, are realized in hardware leading to a fast and efficient implementation. The control flow intensive parts, which often wait for the completion of the calculations, are implemented in software. This allows easier design and maintenance for the parts realized in software, as they are easier to program and debug.

An early design using the HW/SW approach can be found in [64]. It proposes an Arithmetic Logic Unit in hardware, which is controlled by a microcode program, thus, reducing design effort and resource usage compared to a pure hardware design. The decrease in resource usage stems from the fact that the microcode stored in memory replaces the otherwise required finite state machine. In [48] an HW/SW design for the Diffie-Hellman key exchange is introduced. Its authors employ a combination of general purpose processor and FPGA, where the FPGA is used to implement the arithmetic operations and the EC addition and doubling. The scalar multiplication is realized on the general purpose processor. This contrasts with the microcode implementation from [64], which implements only the arithmetic in hardware.

A more elaborate approach is presented in [102]. Its architecture allows the exploitation of several Modular Arithmetic Logical Units in parallel, which are controlled by a microcode program or directly by a general purpose processor. Former variant shortens the communication path and, thus, increases throughput. Using different configurations of this architecture, the authors have realized computations for ECC and HECC[1].

Note that above solutions consider ECC over $\mathbb{GF}(2^m)$ and not over $\mathbb{GF}(p)$ as done in this work. A design for $\mathbb{GF}(p)$ is presented in [101], which consists of one Modular Arithmetic Logical Unit controlled by an 8051 μ-controller. The authors note that this architecture may be used for RSA, too.

HW/SW implementations for just RSA are presented in [28, 117]. Both realize the modular multiplication in hardware, while the exponentiation algorithm is executed in software. In [28], the authors compare this mixed implementation with a pure hardware and a pure software realization of their design concluding that the HW/SW combination is superior to the two other design. The more elaborate design from [117] uses a pipelined approach based on [113] for the modular arithmetic, while the exponentiation is executed on a NIOS soft-core processor. Note that this is somewhat similar to the design proposed in this work. However, because this work also considers ECC, it employs shorter pipelines and parallel modular multipliers, which are not beneficial in the application environment of [117]. Additionally, [117] lacks the on-chip realization of the auxiliary cryptographic function enabling it to execute complete schemes on-chip.

2.3. Single-chip solutions

Single-chip solutions for cryptographic realizations allow the encapsulation of complete cryptographic schemes. This, of course, eases the reuse of such designs, as they contain all the needed functionality and free the host system from the low level control task. Additionally, this approach also increases security by reducing the eavesdropping risk, as the secret data – e.g., private keys – does not have to leave the chip. Thus, an attacker is not able to measure the secret data directly from the circuit paths.

The authors of [17], who offer contemplations on design strategies for secure embedded networking, come to similar conclusions. They also identify better support for long-term security as a special advantage of such integrated co-processors on reconfigurable hardware. This way, it is relatively easy to adjust to new standards and algorithms.

As an early single-chip cryptography solution [73] encapsulates the symmetric cryptographic functionality required for IPSec[2] on an FPGA. The design from [67] provides similar functionality, but exploits the HW/SW approach to decrease the resource usage of the control flow intensive parts by realizing them on-chip in software. [25], in contrast – while also offering IPSec functionality using HW/SW co-design, this time including an RSA core – executes the software off-chip, thus, increasing the eavesdropping risk.

Single-chip solutions more aimed at public key cryptography are presented in [120, 38, 89]. All three are implemented as SoC consisting of a single general purpose processor and several optimized cores for modular arithmetic and for auxiliary functions. Thus, they all apply HW/SW co-design executing the time-critical operations on the optimized

---
[1]Hyperelliptic Curve Cryptography
[2]Internet Protocol Security, see [53]

Chapter 2. Related work

cores, while the general purpose processor is responsible for the control of the different cores utilizing them to compute a cryptographic scheme.

Note that these designs, especially [120], are similar to this work as they also allow the execution of RSA and ECC schemes on a single chip. In contrast to this work, however, parallelization is only considered to a certain degree, the synergies between RSA and ECC are not exploited to the same degree, and the general purpose processors are utilized to a lesser degree.

In [38] a co-processor for secret and public cryptography is introduced. The authors propose a system consisting of several cores for cryptographic functions like RSA, ECC, AES, and hash function. A NIOS soft-core processor is used to control the execution of cryptographic schemes using above cores. In contrast to this work, [38] does not consider parallelization in a significant way. Furthermore, there are separate cores for RSA and ECC, which are only geared to a single bit-width each. They execute a complete modular exponentiation or a point multiplication, respectively, including the control flow intensive parts in hardware. Thus, the design is not as flexible and upgradeable as this work. It does not allow to operate on arbitrary bit-widths required for the desired security level. To change the bit-widths, the design from [38] would have to be modified and synthesized again. Furthermore, it would be more complicated to incorporate a new cryptographic approach like PBC. Note that [38] uses ECC over $\mathbb{GF}(2^m)$, thus, there are no synergies between ECC and RSA on the modular arithmetic level to be exploited as done in this work. Overall, [38] leaves the impression to be build up form separate cores, which, originally, were not intended as part of an integrated cryptographic co-processor.

The design from [89] features a general purpose processor and separate cores for symmetric encryption, RSA/ECC, random number generation, MPEG encoding, and MPEG decoding. Because the aim of the authors was the introduction of a new design methodology and their realization includes MPEG capability, [89] seems to be less suited for pure cryptographic applications than this work. In contrast, this works exhibits a compact single core for the cryptographic auxiliary functions, focuses on the modular operations, and considers parallelization to a larger degree. Finally, the performance of scheme executions is not given in [89]. Thus, comparisons with this work are not possible.

The cryptographic co-processor from [120] is an ASIC design optimized for energy and area featuring a RISC CPU, a core for random number generation, and a core for modular arithmetic. The execution of signature and verification schemes is controlled by the CPU, which uses the hardware cores. The core for modular arithmetic is word-based and may be used for both RSA and ECC up to a bit-length of 2048. This flexibility promises a relatively easy upgradeability for new approaches like PBC as done in this work. In contrast to this work, [120] does not feature cores for symmetric en-/decryption or hash. Furthermore, the algorithms for modular multiplication and elliptic operations are included as microcode in the word-based RSA/ECC core. Finally, the design is aimed for application in clients making the considerations about throughput less important. This may also be the reason that parallelization is included to a smaller degree only.

Chapter 3.
Mathematical foundations

For the understanding and the implementation of public key cryptography, a firm grasp of its mathematical foundations is necessary. Thus, this chapter presents the algebraic structures required by the cryptographic schemes examined in this work. This includes an introduction to the operations in these structures and some additional algorithms.

3.1. Algebraic structures

The cryptographic schemes examined in this work are based on finite groups and/or finite fields. A general definition of these two algebraic structures is provided in the following, while the specifics for their implementation over integers are given later. Note that the definitions are restricted to the information needed in this work. A more thorough introduction to algebraic structures may be found in [41].

3.1.1. Groups

A mathematical group consists of a set of elements and an operation $\circ$ defined over these elements. It is called an *additive* or *multiplicative group*, depending on whether $\circ$ denotes the addition or the multiplication operation, respectively.

Definition 3.1 *A* group *is a non-empty set G with a binary operation $\circ : G \times G \to G$ and the following properties.*

1. *The operation $\circ$ is* associative, *i.e., for all $a, b, c \in G$ it holds that $a \circ (b \circ c) = (a \circ b) \circ c$.*

2. *There exists an* identity *element $e \in G$ such that for all $a \in G$ it holds that $a \circ e = e \circ a = a$.*

3. *For each $a \in G$ there exists an* inverse *element $a^{-1} \in G$ with $a \circ a^{-1} = a^{-1} \circ a = e$.*

In the context of groups the following additional definitions are used in this work.

- G is called an *abelian* or *commutative* group, if the operation $\circ$ is commutative, i.e., for all $a, b \in G$ it holds that $a \circ b = b \circ a$.

Chapter 3. Mathematical foundations

- A group G is called *cyclic*, if it may be generated by a single element $a \in G$, i.e., if $G = \{a^n | n \in \mathbb{N}\}$ holds. The element a is called a *generator of G*.

- The *order of a group* G denoted by $\#G$ is the amount of different elements in the set G. If the amount of elements is infinite, then $\#G = \infty$. The group is called *finite*, if the order of the group is finite.

- The *order of an element* a is defined as the least integer $n \in \mathbb{N}$, for which $a^n = e$ holds. a^n denotes the n-times repeated application of the operation $\circ$. The order of a is referred to as *infinite*, if such an integer n does not exist.

  If G is the cyclic group generated by a, the order of the element a is equal to the order of the group G.

- Let G_1 and G_2 be two groups, where the group operations are defined identically. If $G_1 \subset G_2$ holds, then G_1 is called a *subgroup of G_2*.

3.1.2. Fields

A field F can be seen as a set of elements and the two binary operations addition and multiplication defined over these elements, where the set is an abelian group in respect to each of these operations. An exception is that there exists no multiplicative inverse element for the multiplicative identity element 0, i.e., the division by 0 is not defined. Furthermore, addition and multiplication follow the distributive law.

Definition 3.2 *A field is a non-empty set F with two binary operations $+ : F \times F \to F$ and $\cdot : F \times F \to F$ and the following properties.*

1. *Both operations $+$ and $\cdot$ are* associative*, i.e., for all $a, b, c \in F$ it holds that $a + (b + c) = (a + b) + c$ and $a \cdot (b \cdot c) = (a \cdot b) \cdot c$.*

2. *Both operations $+$ and $\cdot$ are* commutative*, i.e., for all $a, b \in F$ it holds that $a + b = b + a$ and $a \cdot b = b \cdot a$.*

3. *The multiplication $\cdot$ is* distributive *over the addition $+$, i.e., for all $a, b, c \in F$ it holds that $a \cdot (b + c) = (a \cdot b) + (a \cdot c)$.*

4. *There exists an* additive identity element $0 \in F$ *such that for all $a \in F$ it holds that $a + 0 = 0 + a = a$.*

5. *There exists a* multiplicative identity element $1 \in F$ *such that for all $a \in F$ it holds that $a \cdot 1 = 1 \cdot a = a$.*

6. *For each $a \in F$ there exists an* additive inverse element $-a \in F$ *with $(-a) + a = a + (-a) = 0$.*

7. *For each $a \in F$ with $a \neq 0$ there exists a* multiplicative inverse element $a^{-1} \in F$ *with $a^{-1} \cdot a = a \cdot a^{-1} = 1$.*

In the context of fields the following additional definitions are used in this work.

- The *order of a field F* denoted by $\#F$ is the amount of different elements in the set F. If the amount of elements is infinite, then $\#F = \infty$. The field is called *finite*, if the order of the field is finite. Finite fields are also called *Galois Fields*.
- Let F_1 and F_2 be two fields, where addition and multiplication are identically defined. If $F_1 \subset F_2$ holds, then F_1 is called a *subfield of F_2* and F_2 is called an *extension field of F_1*.

3.2. Modular arithmetic

All public key algorithms examined in this work are based on modular arithmetic, which allows them to share a common hardware core. The computations within the modular arithmetic are executed on positive integers x in the range $[0, q-1]$, where q is an integer number depending on the used cryptographic approach. Therefore, the results of operations like addition and multiplication have to be reduced modulo q.

For RSA the modulus is the product of two large prime numbers, thus, the algebraic structure in this case is a multiplicative abelian group. For ECC and PBC q is chosen as a large prime, thus, the algebraic structure the operations work on is the finite field $\mathbb{GF}(q)$. Note that for PBC an additional extension field $\mathbb{GF}(q^k)$ is required. In this work only a simple pairing case is considered utilizing extension fields with the embedding degree $k = 2$. The operations in $\mathbb{GF}(q^2)$ are reviewed in Section 3.4.4.

It is also possible to implement ECC and PBC based on finite fields $\mathbb{GF}(2^m)$ with $m \geq 0$, which are called binary finite fields. Operational units for these fields, however, may not be reused for RSA. Because this work focuses on parallelization, operations in binary fields are not examined. For designs, which have to support calculations in both $\mathbb{GF}(q)$ and $\mathbb{GF}(2^m)$, so called *unified architectures* may be used, see [21, 31].

3.2.1. Modular operations

For a realization the modular operations have to be mapped to actual hardware units. As described in Chapter 6, the elementary computational units in this work operate on words. Thus, long integers must be split into parts of word-length each, which is also called *µ-radix representation*, where $\mu = 2^w$ is the amount of different values one word with the word-length w may represent. In this representation, a long integer a – also called *multi-precision integer* – is stored in n words a_i, for which the following equation holds.

$$a = a_{n-1} \cdot 2^{w(n-1)} + a_{n-2} \cdot 2^{w(n-2)} + \cdots + a_1 \cdot 2^w + a_0$$

Modular addition and subtraction

The algorithms for modular addition and subtraction are relatively straight-forward, because the intermediate result is at most off by $(q-1)$, which may be corrected by simply subtracting or adding q, respectively. This is shown in Algorithm 3.1 and Algorithm 3.2.

Chapter 3. Mathematical foundations

Algorithm 3.1 Modular addition

Input: integers $a, b \in [0, q-1]$, modulus q
Output: integer $c = a + b \mod q$
1: $c := a + b$
2: **if** $c \geq q$ **then**
3: $\quad c := c - q$
4: **end if**
5: **return** c

Algorithm 3.2 Modular subtraction

Input: integers $a, b \in [0, q-1]$, modulus q
Output: integer $c = a - b \mod q$
1: $c := a - b$
2: **if** $c < 0$ **then**
3: $\quad c := c + q$
4: **end if**
5: **return** c

Modular multiplication

The modular multiplication is the most critical modular operation in the examined public key algorithms, mainly because of two reasons. Firstly, it is more complex, because the not-yet-reduced result may have the double bit-length of q. Secondly, it is executed frequently in all considered cryptographic schemes.

Therefore, an extensive body of research concerning the increase in efficiency may be found in literature. Probably the most common algorithm is the Montgomery multiplication, see [80, 74], which is also used in this work and described in more detail in Section 3.2.2. Other important approaches are the Barrett multiplication [7, 74], which may be improved using Quisquater's variant, see [29], and the modular multiplication utilizing reduction for special moduli, e.g., Pseudo-Mersenne primes, see [74]. Other examples are the use of residue number systems, shortly described in Section 4.3.1, and a novel modular multiplication algorithm realized by the author, see [15].

Modular inversion

Because modular division is very difficult, it is usually substituted by a modular multiplication with the multiplicative inverse. However, this inversion is still more expensive than a modular multiplication. Thus, this must be taken into account by the algorithms on higher abstraction levels and leads, e.g., to the use of projective coordinates instead of affine coordinates, see Section 3.3.2.

The modular inverse a^{-1}, with $a^{-1} \cdot a \equiv 1 \mod q$, is usually computed using *Fermat's little theorem* or the *Extended Euclidean algorithm*, see [74]. Former one is composed of modular multiplications only, while latter one uses normal integer operations and exhibits a more complex control flow. However, although the Extended Euclidean algorithm is more resource consuming, it is also more efficient, i.e., faster to compute. Because the inversion is executed only occasionally and the *Extended Euclidean algorithm* does not easily allow resource sharing with the modular arithmetic, the algorithm according to *Fermat's little theorem* is utilized in this work.

Fermat's little theorem states that if q is prime and a and q are relatively prime to each other, then the following equation holds.
$$a^q \equiv a \mod q$$
From this follows that
$$a^{q-2} \equiv a^{-1} \mod q$$
and, thus, the inverse $a^{-1} \mod q$ may be computed by calculating $a^{q-2} \mod q$.

Modular division by 2

A special case of the modular division is the division by 2, which may be calculated efficiently and is required for the elliptic curve point addition and doubling algorithms, see Section 3.3.2. Its computation is based on the fact that for the result c, the following equivalence holds.
$$c + c \equiv a \mod q.$$
However, it may be that $2c > q$, in which case this intermediate result is reduced by q, i.e., $a = 2c - q$. Because q is odd and $2c$ even, this may only the case, if a is also odd. This fact is exploited in Algorithm 3.3.

Algorithm 3.3 Modular division by 2

Input: integer $a \in [0, q-1]$, modulus q
Output: integer $c = a/2 \mod q$
1: **if** a is odd **then**
2: $\quad t = a + q$
3: **else**
4: $\quad t = a$
5: **end if**
6: $c := t \div 2$ {implemented with right-shift by 1 bit}
7: **return** c

Modular exponentiation

The modular exponentiation $c = a^b \mod q$ is realized as sequence of modular multiplications. Because it is an important operation, many different algorithms with different advantages and disadvantages exist, see [36] for a survey. In this work the *Montgomery Powering Ladder* is utilized, as it supports parallel execution, see Section 4.3.3. Therefore, only the most basic algorithm, namely "Square and Multiply" is presented here. This algorithms traverses the exponent b bit-by-bit. For each inspected bit, the intermediate result is squared and for each bit equal to 1 the intermediate result is also multiplied with the base a. This is shown in Algorithm 3.4 in detail.

Chapter 3. Mathematical foundations

Algorithm 3.4 Modular exponentiation "Square and Multiply" (from [74])

Input: base $a \in [0, q-1]$, modulus q, exponent $b \geq 1$ in binary representation with bit-length l (i.e., $b = (b_{l-1}b_{l-2}\ldots b_1 b_0)$)
Output: result $a^b \mod q$
1: $t := 1$
2: **for** $i := l$ downto 0 **do**
3: $\quad t := t \cdot t \mod q$
4: $\quad$ **if** $b_i = 1$ **then**
5: $\quad\quad t := t \cdot a \mod q$
6: $\quad$ **end if**
7: **end for**
8: **return** t

Modular square root

The algorithm for the calculation of a modular square root used in this work is taken from [42]. It provides different sub algorithms for the three cases $q \equiv 3 \mod 4$, $q \equiv 1 \mod 8$, and $q \equiv 5 \mod 8$. However, in this work the square root operation is only needed for the PBC scheme as part of the Hash-to-point operation, see Section 4.4.6. Because the PBC scheme realized in this work is restricted to a simple parameter set, only the case $q \equiv 3 \mod 4$ needs to be considered, see Section 3.4.3. Fortunately, this is the most simple case in which the square root may be computed by calculating a modular exponentiation with the exponent $k+1$, where $4k+3 = q$ holds. Thus, the square root is computed by

$$\sqrt{a} = a^{k+1} \mod q$$

Note that this approach only generates a solution $\sqrt{a}$, if one exists. Thus, to check whether the solution exists, $\sqrt{a}^2 \equiv a \mod q$ should be tested.

3.2.2. Montgomery multiplication

The *Montgomery multiplication*, see [80, 74], is based on the Montgomery reduction, which computes $a \cdot R^{-1} \mod q$, where q is the modulus and $R > q$ is coprime to q. If R is chosen to be a large power of 2, the division can be executed using right shifts, thus, simplifying the reduction operation. Therefore, normally and also in this work, R is set to 2^{wn}, where w denotes the word-width and n refers to the word-count of q. Furthermore, by interleaving the multiplication and reduction phase the amount of necessary memory accesses is reduced. A word-based variant of the Montgomery multiplication is depicted in Algorithm 3.5.

The Montgomery multiplication calculates $ab \cdot R^{-1} \mod q$ instead of $ab \mod q$. To deal with this drawback, the operands have to be transferred into the so called *Montgomery space* before the computations and out of it afterwards. In the Montgomery space an input value a is substituted by aR.

How the computations within the Montgomery space fit together is shown in the

3.2. Modular arithmetic

Algorithm 3.5 Montgomery multiplication (from [74])
Input: factors $a = (a_{n-1}, \ldots, a_1, a_0)$, $b = (b_{n-1}, \ldots, b_1, b_0)$, modulus $q = (q_{n-1}, \ldots, q_1, q_0)$, $q' = -q^{-1} \mod 2^w$, $R = 2^{wn}$
Output: $ab \cdot R^{-1} \mod q$
1: $t := 0$ $\{t = (t_n, t_{n-1}, \ldots, t_1, t_0)\}$
2: **for** $i := 0$ to $n-1$ **do**
3: $\quad u := (t_0 + a_i b_0) q' \mod 2^w$
4: $\quad t := (t + a_i y + uq)/2^w$
5: **end for**
6: **if** $t \geq q$ **then**
7: $\quad t := t - q$
8: **end if**
9: **return** t

following. Thereby, the Montgomery multiplication is denoted by $\bar{\times}$ and values in the Montgomery space are marked as $\bar{a}$. Note that the result of a multiplication of the factors $\bar{a}$ and $\bar{b}$ is again in Montgomery space.

$$\begin{aligned}
\bar{a} \bar{\times} \bar{b} \mod q &= (a \cdot R) \bar{\times} (b \cdot R) \mod q \\
&= a \cdot R \cdot b \cdot R \cdot R^{-1} \mod q \\
&= (ab) \cdot R \mod q \\
&= \overline{ab} \mod q
\end{aligned}$$

This means that conversions into and from Montgomery space are only needed at the beginning and at the end of the computations, respectively. Both conversions may be executed utilizing the Montgomery multiplication:

- For the transformation into the Montgomery space, an integer a is multiplied with $R^2 \mod q$, which has to be precomputed and stored.

$$\begin{aligned}
a \bar{\times} R^2 \mod q &= a \cdot R^2 \cdot R^{-1} \mod q \\
&= a \cdot R \mod q \\
&= \bar{a} \mod q
\end{aligned}$$

- The transformation out of the Montgomery space may be done by a Montgomery multiplication with 1.

$$\begin{aligned}
\bar{a} \bar{\times} 1 \mod q &= \bar{a} \cdot 1 \cdot R^{-1} \mod q \\
&= a \cdot R \cdot R^{-1} \mod q \\
&= a \mod q
\end{aligned}$$

Chapter 3. Mathematical foundations

3.2.3. Chinese Remainder Theorem

The *Chinese Remainder Theorem* (CRT) states that there exists an unique solution modulo $m = \sum_{i=1}^{n} m_i$ for a system of simultaneous congruences

$$a \equiv b_1 \mod m_1$$
$$a \equiv b_2 \mod m_2$$
$$\vdots$$
$$a \equiv b_n \mod m_n,$$

where the moduli m_i are relatively prime to each other. This may be used to improve the modular exponentiation in RSA, where computations are executed modulo $n = p \cdot q$. Furthermore, residue number systems, which offer a possibility to massively parallelize computations with multi-precision integers, are based on the CRT, see Section 4.3.1.

To find the unique solution a for a system of simultaneous congruences, *Gauss*'s or *Garner*'s algorithm may be used. Latter algorithm is more efficient for practical implementations, because its calculations are executed modulo the small moduli, which is less costly for multi-precision integer computations, see [74]. Algorithm 3.6 details Garner's algorithm.

Algorithm 3.6 Garner's algorithm (from [74])

Input: positive integer $m = \sum_{i=1}^{n} m_i$ with m_i relatively prime to each other, modular representation $(b_1, b_2, \ldots, b_n)$ for a
Output: positive multi-precision integer a
1: **for** $i := 2$ to n **do**
2:     $C_i := 1$
3:     **for** $j := 1$ to $i - 1$ **do**
4:        $t := m_j^{-1} \mod m_i$
5:        $C_i := t \cdot C_i \mod m_i$
6:     **end for**
7: **end for**
8: $t := b_1$, $a := t$
9: **for** $0 := 2$ to n **do**
10:     $t := (b_i - a) \cdot C_i \mod m_i$
11:     $a := a + t \cdot \prod_{j=1}^{i-1} \cdot m_j$
12: **end for**
13: **return** a

3.3. Elliptic curve group

This section offers a short introduction to *elliptic curves* (EC), sufficient for the understanding of this work. For more information, see [12, 39].

3.3. Elliptic curve group

An elliptic curve is defined over a finite field and can be used as foundation for public key algorithms. Although an elliptic curve may be defined over both $\mathbb{GF}(q)$ or $\mathbb{GF}(2^m)$, only former case is considered and explained here.

An elliptic curve E is a set of points $P = (x, y)$, where the coordinates $x, y \in \mathbb{GF}(q)$ satisfy the *Weierstraß*-equation

$$y^2 = x^3 + ax + b.$$

The *Weierstraß*-coefficients $a, b \in \mathbb{GF}(q)$ must satisfy $4a^3 + 27b^2 \not\equiv 0 \mod q$.

Together with a point at infinity denoted $\mathcal{O}$ as identity element the points of such an elliptic curve E form an additive abelian group called $E(\mathbb{GF}(q))$. As shown in Figure 3.1(a) the addition $R = P+Q$ may be interpreted geometrically. For the case $P = Q$ a special doubling operation is needed, because the calculation of the gradient would result in a division by 0. Its geometrical interpretation is depicted in Figure 3.1(b).

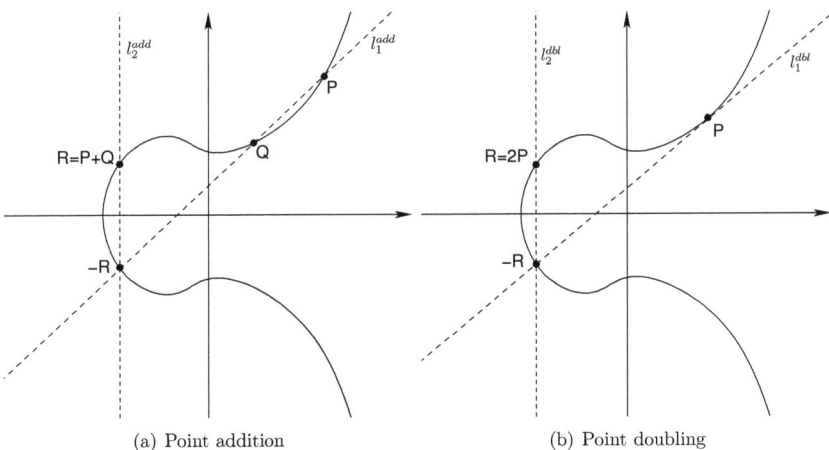

(a) Point addition (b) Point doubling

Figure 3.1.: Geometric interpretation of point addition and doubling

The first step is to draw the line l_1^{add} through the points P and Q or the tangent l_1^{dbl} to the curve at point P, respectively. The point of intersection with the curve E is the negative of the resulting point R, which, in turn, is found as the point of intersection between E and the line l_2^{add} or l_2^{dbl}, respectively. If l_1^{add} or l_1^{dbl} are parallel to the Y-axis, the resulting point is defined as the point at infinity $\mathcal{O}$. The amount of points on the curve $E(\mathbb{GF}(q))$ is called *order of the curve* E and is denoted $\#E(\mathbb{GF}(q))$.

Note that for cryptographic applications only the points of a cyclic subgroup of E with a generator point G are used. To ensure a suitable security level, the order of this subgroup n – which is also the order of the generator point G – must be a prime number with a large enough bit-length. The relation between the order of the curve $\#E(\mathbb{GF}(q))$ and the order of the subgroup n is given by $\#E(\mathbb{GF}(q)) = h \cdot n$, where h is denoted *cofactor*. For ECC, n and q should have a similar bit-length and the cofactor should be a very small integer, i.e., $h = 1$ in the best case. For PBC q and h may be larger than n.

3.3.1. Additive operations in affine coordinates

The 2-dimensional coordinates used in above geometric representation are called *affine coordinates*. The concrete algorithms for addition and doubling of points are composed of modular operations and shown in the following.

In the general case the addition of the points $P = (x_P, y_P)$ and $Q = (x_Q, y_Q)$ results in the point $R = (x_R, y_R)$ as follows.

$$s = \frac{y_P - y_Q}{x_P - x_Q}$$
$$x_R = s^2 - x_P - x_Q$$
$$y_R = -y_P + s \cdot (x_P - x_R)$$

In the doubling case $P = Q$ the resulting point R may be computed as follows.

$$s = \frac{3x_P^2 - a}{2y_P}$$
$$x_R = s^2 - 2x_P$$
$$y_R = -y_P + s \cdot (x_P - x_R).$$

Note that from $\mathcal{O} = P + (-P) = (x_P, y_P) + (x_P, -y_P)$ follows that the negative of a point $P = (x_P, y_P)$ can be computed by toggling the sign of y_P, i.e., $-P = (x_P, -y_P)$.

Because the points of E compose an additive abelian group, there is no multiplication operation between points. However, the repetitive addition of a point onto itself is called point multiplication, see Section 3.3.3

3.3.2. Additive operations in projective coordinates

Both algorithms for point addition and doubling in affine coordinates need one modular inversion each, which is a very costly operation. To avoid this, alternative coordinate systems with additional coordinates were proposed. Their basic idea is to keep track of numerators and denominators separately and to execute the inversion only once at the end. In this work the *Jacobian projective coordinates* are used – in the following called *projective coordinates*. An overview on other common coordinate systems is given in [24].

3.3. Elliptic curve group

Algorithm 3.7 Algorithm for point addition (from [42])
Input: $P_0 = (x_0, y_0, z_0)$, $P_1 = (x_1, y_1, z_1)$, *Weierstraß*-coefficients a, b
Output: projective coordinates of point $P_2 = P_0 + P_1 = (x_2, y_2, z_2)$
1: $t_1 := x_0$, $t_2 := y_0$
2: **if** ($z_1 \neq 1$) **then**
3:     $t_7 := z_1^2$ {SQR1}
4:     $t_1 := t_1 \cdot t_7$ {MULT2}
5:     $t_7 := z_1 \cdot t_7$ {MULT3}
6:     $t_2 := t_2 \cdot t_7$ {MULT4}
7: **end if**
8: $t_7 := z_0^2$ {SQR5}
9: $t_4 := x_1 \cdot t_7$ {MULT6}
10: $t_7 := z_0 \cdot t_7$ {MULT7}
11: $t_5 := y_1 \cdot t_7$ {MULT8}
12: $t_4 := t_1 - t_4$ {SUB9}
13: $t_5 := t_2 - t_5$ {SUB10}
14: **if** ($t_4 = 0$) **then**
15:     **if** ($t_5 = 0$) **then**
16:        $x_2 := 0$; $y_2 := 0$; $z_2 := 0$ and HALT
17:     **else**
18:        $x_2 := 1$; $y_2 := 1$; $z_2 := 0$ and HALT
19:     **end if**
20: **end if**
21: $t_1 := 2 \cdot t_1 - t_4$ {MULT11_ADD and SUB12}
22: $t_2 := 2 \cdot t_2 - t_5$ {MULT13_ADD and SUB14}
23: **if** ($z_1 \neq 1$) **then**
24:     $t_3 := z_0 \cdot z_1$ {MULT15}
25: **else**
26:     $t_3 := z_0$
27: **end if**
28: $z_2 := t_3 \cdot t_4$ {MULT16}
29: $t_7 := t_4^2$ {SQR17}
30: $t_4 := t_4 \cdot t_7$ {MULT18}
31: $t_7 := t_1 \cdot t_7$ {MULT19}
32: $t_1 := t_5^2$ {SQR20}
33: $x_2 := t_1 - t_7$ {SUB21}
34: $t_7 := t_7 - 2 \cdot x_2$ {MULT22_ADD and SUB23}
35: $t_5 := t_5 \cdot t_7$ {MULT24}
36: $t_4 := t_2 \cdot t_4$ {MULT25}
37: $t_2 := t_5 - t_4$ {SUB26}
38: $y_2 := t_2 \div 2$ {DIV27}
39: **return** $P_2 = (x_2, y_2, z_2)$

Chapter 3. Mathematical foundations

The transformation between affine coordinates (x_P, y_P) and projective coordinates (x'_P, y'_P, z'_P) may be done according to the following equations.

$$x_P = \frac{x'_P}{(z'_P)^2}, y_P = \frac{y'_P}{(z'_P)^3}$$

Note that this representation is not unique, because

$$(x'_P, y'_P, z'_P) = (a^2 x'_P, a^3 y'_P, a z'_P)$$

for all $a \in \mathbb{GF}(q) \backslash \{0\}$. From this follows that affine coordinates may be easily transferred to projective coordinates by setting $x' = x$, $y' = y$, and $z' = 1$. The point at infinity $\mathcal{O}$ has the coordinates $(a^2, a^3, 0)$ for all nonzero a. For simplicity it is defined as $(1, 1, 0)$.

Algorithm 3.8 Algorithm for point doubling for curves with $a = -3$ (from [39])

Input: $P_1 = (x_1, y_1, z_1)$, *Weierstraß*-coefficient b
Output: projective coordinates for point $P_2 = 2 \cdot P_1 = (x_2, y_2, z_2)$
1: **if** ($y_1 = 0$ or $z_1 = 0$) **then**
2: $\quad x_2 := 1; y_2 := 1; z_2 := 0$ and HALT
3: **end if**
4: $t_1 := z_1^2$ {SQR1}
5: $t_2 := x_1 - t_1$ {SUB2}
6: $t_1 := x_1 + t_1$ {ADD3}
7: $t_2 := t_2 \cdot t_1$ {MULT4}
8: $t_2 := 3 \cdot t_2$ {MULT5_ADD}
9: $t_4 := 2 \cdot y_1$ {MULT6_ADD}
10: $z_2 := t_4 \cdot z_1$ {MULT7}
11: $t_4 := t_4^2$ {SQR8}
12: $t_3 := y_3 \cdot x_1$ {MULT9}
13: $t_4 := t_4^2$ {SQR10}
14: $t_4 := t_4 \div 2$ {DIV11}
15: $t_4 := t_2^2$ {SQR12}
16: $t_1 := 2 \cdot t_3$ {MULT13_ADD}
17: $x_2 := x_2 - t_1$ {SUB14}
18: $t_1 := t_3 - x_2$ {SUB15}
19: $t_1 := t_1 \cdot t_2$ {MULT16}
20: $y_2 := t_1 - t_4$ {SUB17}
21: **return** $P_2 = (x_2, y_2, z_2)$

The use of projective coordinates results, of course, in different algorithms for point addition and doubling. These are shown in Algorithm 3.7 and Algorithm 3.8, respectively. For better readability the projective coordinates are not marked with ' anymore. To better distinguish between the operations, they are numbered serially. Multiplications with small constants like *MULT11_ADD* are substituted with one or several subsequent additions for efficiency, which is reflected by the naming scheme.

Note that Algorithm 3.8 is intended for a special case, where the *Weierstraß*-coefficient $a = -3$. This allows a faster doubling operations on special curves used in this work, see Section 7.1, and does not sacrifice security. An algorithm for point doubling in the general case may be found in [42].

3.3.3. Point multiplication

The *point multiplication* – also called *scalar multiplication* or *EC multiplication* – is a repetitive addition of a point onto itself. Thus, the point multiplication kP with $k \in \mathbb{N}$ is defined as

$$kP = \underbrace{P + P + \ldots + P}_{k-times}.$$

This is similar to the (modular) exponentiation, with the difference that the exponentiation uses multiplicative group operations, while the point multiplication utilizes additive group operations. Thus, the counterpart to the "Square and Multiply" exponentiation algorithm, see Algorithm 3.4, is the "Double and Add" point multiplication. For this, all multiplications and squarings are substituted by additions and doublings, respectively. Using the same approach all other algorithms for (modular) exponentiation may also be utilized for point multiplication.

3.4. Pairings

Originally, pairings were used in cryptography as tool of cryptanalysts to decrease the complexity of possible attacks. But in recent years they were also employed as foundation of the relatively new *pairing-based cryptography* (PBC).

This section offers a short overview on the necessary mathematical background, which allows a basic understanding of the scheme presented in Section 4.1.3. For more information, see for example [13, 70].

The most common pairings in literature are the *Weil pairing* and the *Tate pairing*. Because the implementation of latter pairing is usually more efficient, only the Tate pairing is considered in this work.

3.4.1. General pairings

Generally, schemes of pairing-based cryptography are independent from the actual pairing variant, if the pairing exhibits certain properties, see [13]. In this context a pairing is a bilinear function

$$e : G_1 \times G_2 \to G_3.$$

G_1 and G_2 are additive abelian groups, whose elements have the order n, i.e., for all $P \in G_1$ it holds that $nP = \mathcal{O}_{G_1}$ and for all $Q \in G_2$ it holds that $nQ = \mathcal{O}_{G_2}$, where $\mathcal{O}_{G_1}$ and $\mathcal{O}_{G_2}$ are the additive identity elements of the groups G_1 and G_2, respectively. G_3 is a multiplicative cyclic group with order n. Furthermore, the pairing satisfies two additional properties:

Chapter 3. Mathematical foundations

Bilinearity For all $P, P' \in G_1$ and $Q, Q' \in G_2$ the equations $e(P+P', Q) = e(P,Q)e(P',Q)$ and $e(P, Q+Q') = e(P,Q)e(P,Q')$ hold.

Non-degeneracy

- For all $P \in G_1$, where $P \neq \mathcal{O}_{G_1}$, there exists $Q \in G_2$ with $e(P,Q) \neq 1$.
- For all $Q \in G_2$, where $Q \neq \mathcal{O}_{G_2}$, there exists $P \in G_1$ with $e(P,Q) \neq 1$.

From the property of bilinearity follows:

- $e(P, \mathcal{O}_{G_2}) = e(\mathcal{O}_{G_1}, Q) = 1$, because $e(P,Q) = e(P + \mathcal{O}_{G_1}, Q) = e(P,Q)e(\mathcal{O}_{G_1}, Q)$
- $e(-P, Q) = e(P, Q)^{-1} = e(P, -Q)$, because $1 = e(\mathcal{O}_{G_1}, Q) = e(P + (-P), Q) = e(P,Q)e(-P,Q)$
- $e(jP, Q) = e(P, Q)^j = e(P, jQ)$ for all $j \in \mathbb{Z}$

3.4.2. Tate pairing

The Tate pairing is implemented using Miller's algorithm, see [76], which is shown in Algorithm 3.9 in a variant from [70]. It expects the points $P \in G_1 = E(\mathbb{GF}(q))$ and $Q \in G_2 = E(\mathbb{GF}(q^k))$ as input values and uses a basic "Double and Add" approach to produce an element of the extension field $G_3 = \mathbb{GF}(q^k)$.

Algorithm 3.9 Miller's Algorithm (according to [70])

Input: point $P \in E(\mathbb{GF}(q))$, point $Q \in E(\mathbb{GF}(q^k))$
Output: pairing $e(P,Q) \in \mathbb{GF}(q^k)$
1: choose suitable point $S \in E(\mathbb{GF}(q^k))$ {choose S randomly or $S := Q$ [13, page 197]}
2:   $Q' := Q + S$
3:   $T = P$
4:   $f := 1$
5: **for** $i := \lceil \log_2(n) \rceil - 1$ to 0 **do**
6:     compute lines l_1^{dbl}, l_2^{dbl} for the doubling of T
7:     $T := 2T$
8:     compute $f := f^2 \frac{l_1^{dbl}(Q')l_2^{dbl}(S)}{l_1^{dbl}(S)l_2^{dbl}(Q')}$
9:     **if** $n_i = 1$ **then**
10:       compute lines l_1^{add}, l_2^{add} for the addition $T + P$
11:       $T := T + P$
12:       compute $f := f \frac{l_1^{add}(Q')l_2^{add}(S)}{l_1^{add}(S)l_2^{add}(Q')}$
13:     **end if**
14: **end for**
15: **return** f

$l_1^{dbl}(Q')$ denotes the evaluation of the point Q' at the line l_1^{dbl}. The derivation of the necessary equation is beyond the scope of this work, but can be found in [70, 46]. The line equations for the doubling $R = 2T$ with $R = (x_R, y_R, z_R)$ and $T = (x_T, y_T, z_T)$ are as follows.

$$l_1^{dbl}(\mathbf{x}, \mathbf{y}) = (z_R z_T^2 \mathbf{y} - 2y_T^2) - (3x_T^2 + az_T^4)(z_T^2 \mathbf{x} - x_T)$$
$$l_2^{dbl}(\mathbf{x}, \mathbf{y}) = z_R^2 \mathbf{x} - x_R$$

The line equations for the addition $R = T + P$ with $R = (x_R, y_R, z_R)$, $T = (x_T, y_T, z_T)$, and $P = (x_P, y_P, z_P)$ are given as:

$$l_1^{dbl}(\mathbf{x}, \mathbf{y}) = z_R(\mathbf{y} - y_P) - (y_P z_T^3 - y_T)(\mathbf{x} - x_P)$$
$$l_2^{dbl}(\mathbf{x}, \mathbf{y}) = z_R^2 \mathbf{x} - x_R$$

For the evaluation of a point at a line, the coordinates $(\mathbf{x}, \mathbf{y})$ of the point are put into the corresponding line equation.

Note that the result f of Algorithm 3.9 is only defined up to a multiple by an n-th power in $\mathrm{GF}(q^k)$. Therefore, f is raised to the power $(q^k - 1)/n$, which eliminates all n-th powers and provides an unique final value.

3.4.3. Variant of Tate pairing used in this work

Because the focus of this work does not lie on PBC in general, it is restricted to a simple case taken from [13, page 204] using supersingular curves with the embedding degree $k = 2$. Only such curves $E(\mathrm{GF}(q))$ are considered, where $q \equiv 3 \mod 4$ holds and which satisfy the *Weierstraß*-equation of $y^2 = x^3 + x$, i.e., with the *Weierstraß*-coefficients $a = 1$ and $b = 0$. Then the curve order is $\#E(\mathrm{GF}(q)) = q + 1$ and the structure of the curve $E(\mathrm{GF}(q^2))$ over the extension field is $(\mathbb{Z}/(q+1)\mathbb{Z})^2$, i.e., can be expressed as extension field $\mathrm{GF}(q^2) = \mathrm{GF}(q) \cup \{i\}$, where $i = \sqrt{-1}$. This also means that $\#E(\mathrm{GF}(q^2)) = (q+1)^2$.

Finally, as described in [13] a distortion map $\phi : E(\mathrm{GF}(q^k)) \to E(\mathrm{GF}(q^k))$ may be used to define symmetric pairings utilizing the Tate pairing. For this, ϕ is used to map a point on the curve $E(\mathrm{GF}(q))$ to a point on the curve $E(\mathrm{GF}(q^k))$[1], so it can be used as input Q in Algorithm 3.9. This allows on the one hand to use points on the curve $E(\mathrm{GF}(q))$ as both inputs. On the other hand, the distortion map restricts the pairing to a cyclic subgroup of $\mathrm{GF}(q^k)$. Thus, if $R, S \in E(\mathrm{GF}(q))$, $m \in \mathbb{N}$ and $S = mR$, then the following equation holds.

$$e(S, \phi(R)) = e(mR, \phi(R)) = e(R, m\phi(R)) = e(R, \phi(S))$$

The distortion map used in the work is defined as $\phi : (x, y) \to (-x, iy)$, see [13, page 204].

---
[1] Note that a point on $E(\mathrm{GF}(q))$ may be used as input of ϕ, because every point on $E(\mathrm{GF}(q))$ is also a point on $E(\mathrm{GF}(q^k))$, just with all dimensions except the first set to 0.

3.4.4. Operations in the extension field

Some of the calculations in Miller's algorithm have to be executed in the extension field, which is strictly speaking $\mathbb{GF}(q^2) = \mathbb{GF}(q) \cup \{i\}$ with $i = \sqrt{-1}$ in this work. An element f of this extension field can be represented by $f = a + bi$ with $a, b \in \mathbb{GF}(q)$. Operations between the elements $f_1, f_2 \in \mathbb{GF}(q^2)$ of the extension field may be mapped to modular operations in $\mathbb{GF}(q)$. How this is done for the different operations is explained in the following. Note that in the following all operations between $a_{(i)}$ and $b_{(i)}$ are modular operations in $\mathbb{GF}(q)$, although this is omitted for better readability.

Multiplication

The mapping of the multiplication in the extension field may be done straight forward. With help of the Karatsuba multiplication the number of multiplications in $\mathbb{GF}(q)$ may be reduced to three at the cost of an increase in additions. This is shown in the last of the following equations.

$$\begin{aligned} f_1 \cdot f_2 &= (a_1 + b_1 i) \cdot (a_2 + b_2 i) \\ &= a_1 a_2 + a_1 b_2 i + a_2 a_1 i + b_1 b_2 i^2 \\ &= (a_1 a_2 - b_1 b_2) + (a_1 b_2 + a_2 a_1) i \\ &= (a_1 a_2 - b_1 b_2) + [(a_1 + b_1)(a_2 + b_2) - a_1 a_2 - b_1 b_2] i \end{aligned}$$

Squaring

The squaring operation is provided independently from the general multiplication, because it may be realized more efficiently. The corresponding algorithm utilizing modular operations is shown in the following. Note that the equation in the last line requires only two modular multiplications, if the doubling is executed using an addition.

$$\begin{aligned} f^2 = f \cdot f &= (a + bi) \cdot (a + bi) \\ &= a^2 + 2abi + b^2 i^2 \\ &= a^2 - b^2 + 2abi \\ &= (a + b)(a - b) + 2abi \end{aligned}$$

Inversion

Because the inversion in the extension field needs one inversion in $\mathbb{GF}(q)$, it is computationally expensive. Therefore, it is usually used only at the end to calculate the final result. It may be executed with operations in $\mathbb{GF}(q)$ as follows.

$$\begin{aligned} f^{-1} &= (a+bi)^{-1} \\ &= \frac{1}{a+bi} \\ &= \frac{a-bi}{(a+bi)(a-bi)} \\ &= \frac{a-bi}{a^2+b^2} \\ &= \frac{a}{a^2+b^2} + \frac{-b}{a^2+b^2}i \\ &= a \cdot (a^2+b^2)^{-1} - bi \cdot (a^2+b^2)^{-1} \end{aligned}$$

Exponentiation

For the exponentiation in the extension field any algorithm used for the modular exponentiation may be utilized. For this, the modular multiplication and squaring operations have to be substituted with the corresponding operations in the extension field.

Chapter 4.
Cryptographic aspects

In today's telecommunication infrastructure a large amount of communication is done via electronic and insecure channels. In this context, insecure means that the channels are not secure from eavesdropping and that it is possible to substitute transported data with different data. Thus, to enable secure communication, which is necessary for many applications, e.g., business transactions, the communication protocols must include cryptography as a building block. According to [108], security is defined by the following properties:

Confidentiality Except for the sender and the receiver of a message, nobody should be able to read this message. This is usually done by *encrypting* the message – which is also called *plaintext* – into unreadable code – which is also called *ciphertext* – before it is send. The receiver then *decrypts* the ciphertext to recover the original message.

Authentication The receiver should be able to infer the sender of a message, i.e., it should not be possible for an intruder to masquerade himself as somebody else.

Integrity The receiver of a message should be able to perceive any modification of the original message. Thus, it should not be possible for an intruder to replace a genuine message – as whole or partially – with a false message.

Non-Repudiation For the sender of a message it should not be possible to falsely dispute that he is the sender of that message.

Although it is possible to use completely different en-/decryption algorithms for every user pair, the common approach is to parametrize these operations with *keys*. This allows all users to utilize the same cryptographic algorithms, while only users possessing the proper keys are able to read the plaintext. Furthermore, because the cryptographic algorithms are publicly known, they may be extensively examined for possible vulnerabilities.

In the so called *secret key* or *symmetric cryptography* both sender and receiver must possess the same key. However, because nobody else must know this key, a problem for the initial key exchange between both parties arises. As they do not yet have a common key, they can not communicate confidentially. Thus, the key has to be established using a different communication channel, e.g., a personal meeting.

Chapter 4. Cryptographic aspects

To solve this key exchange problem, *public key* or *asymmetric cryptography* was introduced. In this approach every user possesses a key pair consisting of a *public key* and a *private key*. The public key can only be utilized to encrypt a message, while an encrypted message can only be decrypted using the private key. Therefore, the public key may be known to anybody, as it can not be used to decrypt the ciphertext. The private key, however, must be kept confidential by the owner of the key pair.

Public key cryptography may also be utilized to ensure the additional properties authentication, integrity, and non-repudiation. For this, the sender may utilize his private key to *sign* a message. Then, the receiver may *verify* the signature using the public key[1]. Because a valid signature can only be created with the knowledge of the private key and only the sender knows this private key, the receiver can be sure that the message is legitimate.

Note that above descriptions are very superficial. To provide a framework withstanding attacks both on a theoretical and on a practical level, additional problems have to be solved. However, a more thorough introduction is beyond the scope of this work and may be found in [108].

Furthermore, there are many possible realization variants for en-/decryption in both secret and public key cryptography. For public key cryptography, this work covers only the most common, namely, *RSA* and *elliptic curve cryptography* (ECC), and the not so well-known *paring-based cryptography* (PBC). These are described in more detail in the following. Secret key cryptography is considered only as part of public key schemes. In this context, the block cipher AES is used, which is shortly described in Section 4.4.1.

4.1. Public key cryptography

As described above, public key cryptography was introduced to solve the difficulties arising from the exchange of keys. Although there are many proposals for public key algorithms, they all share a basic relationship between private and public key. After the private key is chosen – often randomly – an *one-way* function is used to derive the public key from the private key. Such a function has the property that it is relatively easy to compute in one direction, but computational infeasible in the other direction. Because of this *one-way*-property, the private key may not be derived from the public key.

The first fully-fledged and still most common system is RSA. Also well-known is ECC, which has outgrown its research phase some years ago and now gains a foothold in industry after the introduction of several standards.

Both RSA and ECC are based on modular arithmetic. This similarity of ECC to RSA may be one of the reasons for its success, as the well-researched background of RSA lends some credibility to the security of ECC. Compared to RSA, ECC has the advantage that it uses numbers with shorter bit-lengths and, therefore, its operations are faster to calculate. However, ECC has a more complex mathematical background, which requires the study and realization of more algorithms by the implementer.

---

[1] Note that there are algorithms allowing just en-/decryption or just signing/verifying. However, it seems that only systems allowing both applications are used in practice.

The third public key algorithm covered in this work is PBC, which has not yet outgrown its research phase. Its main application are identity-based schemes, which promise a further simplification of the key exchange problem. This is because the public key may be derived from some unique identifier, e.g., an email-address. Thus, the public key must not be transmitted at all. PBC is based on similar mathematical foundations as used in ECC. Therefore, the research community hopes that it shows itself as resistant to attacks as ECC. Furthermore, many optimizations developed for ECC may be reused in PBC.

This was also the main reason PBC was chosen in this work as third public key algorithm besides RSA and ECC. The hardware core calculating the modular arithmetic may be utilized for all three approaches. Furthermore, some of the algorithms working with modular operations are needed in all three approaches and, thus, may be reused.

Note that all three public key algorithms get their security from a complex mathematical problem, which bestows the one-way function its special property. However, in all three cases, the complexity of the problem has not yet been proven or disproven. But because after years of cryptanalysis no solution for the respective problem is known, the algorithms are believed to be secure.

4.1.1. RSA

Notation for RSA

p, q	prime factors for RSA; large primes with equal bit-length
n	RSA modulus; $n = pq$
e	RSA public exponent; positive integer relatively prime to $(p-1)(q-1)$
d	RSA private exponent; positive integer with $d = e^{-1} \mod ((p-1)(q-1))$
M	message; bit string of arbitrary length
m	message representative; positive integer with $m \in [0, n-1]$
c	ciphertext; positive integer with $c \in [0, n-1]$
s	signature; positive integer with $s \in [0, n-1]$
dp	p's CRT exponent; $dp = d \mod (p-1)$
dq	q's CRT exponent; $dq = d \mod (q-1)$
q_{inv}	q's CRT coefficient; $q_{inv} = q^{-1} \mod p$
(n, e)	public key; consists of modulus n and public exponent e
(n, d)	private key; consists of modulus n and private exponent d

RSA was introduced in [96]. This work utilizes it according to the standard described in [100]. The security of RSA stems from the *integer factorization problem*. Thus, although it is easy to calculate the product of large numbers, it is computational infeasible to find the prime factors of a large number n, which are p and q in case of RSA. The fastest known solution for the factoring problem is the *Number Field Sieve*, see [82].

For the creation of a key pair, two large primes p and q with equal bit length are randomly chosen. The product of these numbers is defined as $n = pq$. As depicted in Table 7.2, typical bit-lengths for n are 1024 and longer. The public exponent e is chosen

Chapter 4. Cryptographic aspects

randomly and relatively prime to $(p-1)(q-1)$. Then, the private exponent is calculated such that $ed \equiv 1 \mod ((p-1)(q-1))$ holds.

The public key contains the modulus[2] n and the public exponent e. In a simple form, the private key consists of the modulus n and the private modulus d. The private key may also be given in an extended form, which allows an optimization using the Chinese Remainder Theorem as described in Section 7.5.4. Then, it also contains the prime factors p and q, the CRT exponents dp and dq, and the CRT coefficient q_{inv}. Note that in the following the private key is given in the not extended form for simplicity.

The basic operation to encrypt the plaintext m into the ciphertext c is

$$c = m^e \mod n.$$

Since d is the multiplicative inverse of e modulo $((p-1)(q-1))$, the decryption operation may be computed by

$$m = c^d \mod n.$$

Because RSA is relatively old and in spite of extensive research no possibility for an attack was found, it features a high confidence in its security. Furthermore, it is relatively easy to understand and implement and its computation is not prohibitive expensive.

According to [57], the public exponent e may be chosen as $2^{16} + 1 =$ 0x00010001 without sacrificing security. This accelerates the encryption and verification operation without decelerating decryption and signing. Therefore, the public exponent e is also called *short exponent* and the private exponent d is also called *long exponent* in this work.

Although no short-cut is known for the basic en-/decryption operation, they alone do not provide sufficient security. For example chosen-ciphertext or dictionary attacks would still be possible. Therefore, the cryptographic schemes use operations like padding, hash function, and random number generation to modify the plaintext before encrypting it with the basic encryption operation. This way, the same plaintext is encrypted into different ciphertexts each time, thus, not allowing direct conclusions from the ciphertext to the plaintext.

RSA Encryption and Decryption (RSAES-OAEP)

The *RSA Encryption Scheme with Optimal Asymmetric Encryption Padding* (RSAES-OAEP) uses the OAEP encoding method to randomize the message before encryption. This way, the actually deterministic RSA encryption is transformed into a probabilistic one. Furthermore, OAEP makes the encryption scheme secure against chosen-ciphertext attacks.

The OAEP encoding operation uses the *mask generation function* (MGF) from [100]. Such a function takes a seed of arbitrary lengths as input and deterministically generates a bit string of the desired length. Additionally, the MGF is pseudo-random, i.e., without knowledge of the seed, it is infeasible to compute any portion of the output.

---

[2]Note that while n is published, p and q must stay secret.

4.1. Public key cryptography

The encryption operation is shown in Algorithm 4.1. It encrypts the message M with the public key (n, e). The label L is an optional input introduced in [100], which is set to the empty string, if it is not provided. Note that RSAES-OAEP is only able to encrypt messages with a length of up to $|n| - 2hLen - 2$ bytes, where $|n|$ is the length of n in bytes and $hLen$ is the output length of the hash function in bytes.

Algorithm 4.1 RSAES-OAEP encryption operation (according to [100])

Input: recipient's RSA public key (n, e), message M, *optional*: label L
Output: ciphertext c
1: **if** label L is not provided **then** let L be the empty string
2: $lHash := \text{Hash}(L)$
3: apply *OAEP encoding* (Figure 4.1): $m := \text{OAEP}_{\text{Encode}}(lHash, M)$
4: $c = m^e \mod n$
5: **return** c

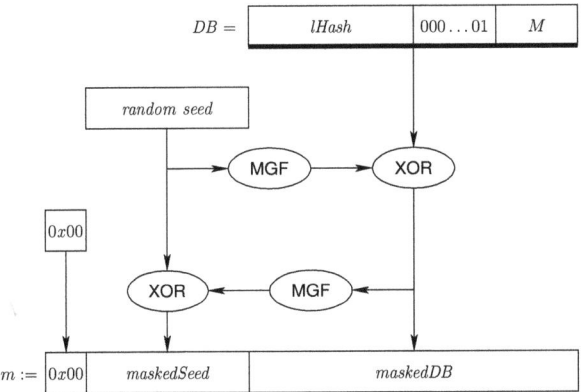

Figure 4.1.: Outline of the OAEP encoding (from [100])

The decryption operation is depicted in Algorithm 4.2. It may be utilized to regain the message M from the ciphertext c using the private key (n, d).

RSA Signature and Verification (RSASSA-PSS)

The *RSA Signature Scheme with Appendix - Probabilistic Signature Scheme* (RSASSA-PSS) exploits the PSS encoding method to introduce randomness into the signature operation. For this, a number called *salt* is randomly chosen and used to modify the message representative. This way, two signatures for the same message are different and the scheme is provable secure, see [100]. The MGF needed for the PSS encoding and verification the same as utilized in the OAEP en-/decoding.

Chapter 4. Cryptographic aspects

Algorithm 4.2 RSAES-OAEP decryption operation (according to [100])

Input: recipient's RSA private key (n, d), ciphertext c, *optional*: label L
Output: message M
1: **if** label L is not provided **then** let L be the empty string
2: $lHash := \text{Hash}(L)$
3: $m := c^d \mod n$
4: apply *OAEP decoding* (Figure 4.2): $(lHash', M) := \text{OAEP}_{\text{Decode}}(m)$
5: **if** $lHash' = lHash$ **then**
6:    **return** message M
7: **else**
8:    **return** *decryption error*
9: **end if**

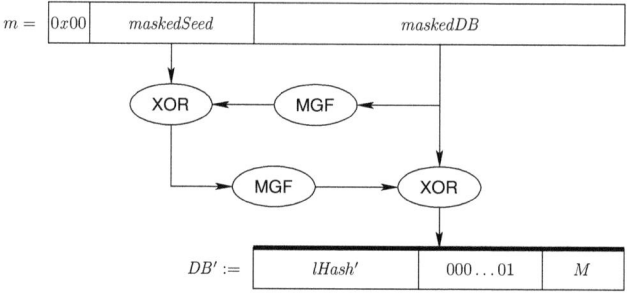

Figure 4.2.: Outline of the OAEP decoding (from [100])

The operation for the signature generation is shown in Algorithm 4.3. Using the private key (n, d) it generates a signature s for a message M of arbitrary length.

Algorithm 4.3 RSASSA-PSS signature operation (according to [100])

Input: signer's RSA private key (n, d), message M
Output: signature s
1: apply *PSS encoding* (Figure 4.3): $m := \text{PSS}_{\text{Encode}}(M)$
2: $s := m^d \mod n$
3: **return** s

The signature verification operation is depicted in Algorithm 4.4. It calculates, whether the signature s is valid for the message M and the public key (n, e).

4.1. Public key cryptography

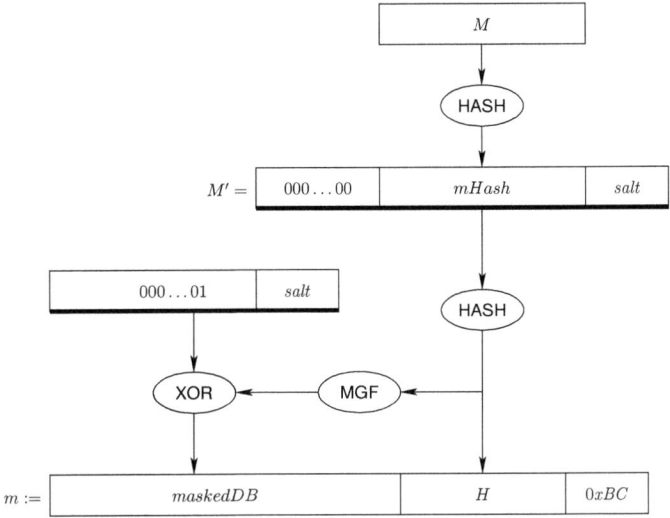

Figure 4.3.: Outline of the PSS encoding (from [100])

4.1.2. Elliptic curve cryptography

Notation for ECC

q	prime number; size and modulus of the underlying finite field $\mathbb{GF}(q)$
a, b	coefficients of the Weierstraß equation; $a, b \in \mathbb{GF}(q)$
G	generator point generating a cyclic subgroup with order n; $G \in E$
E	elliptic curve over $\mathbb{GF}(q)$
$\#E$	order of the curve E
n	prime divisor of $\#E$ and order of G
h	cofactor to n; $h = \#E/n$
x	private key; positive integer with $x \in [0, n-1]$
Q	public key; point on E with $Q = xG$
M	message; bit string of arbitrary length
(c, d)	signature; tuple of two positive integers with $c, d \in [0, n-1]$
(V, c, t)	ciphertext; tri-tuple of point $V \in E$, bit string c, and authentication tag t

Elliptic curve cryptography was developed independently from each other in [77, 56]. It uses the additive group consisting of points on an elliptic curve as described in Section 3.3. The security of this approach stems from the *elliptic curve discrete logarithm problem*. Thus, given the point $P \in E(\mathbb{GF}(q))$ and an integer $x \in [0, n-1]$, it is relatively easy to compute the point multiplication $Q = xP$. However, given the points $P, Q \in E(\mathbb{GF}(q))$, it is computational infeasible to find the integer x with $xP = Q$. The

---
Algorithm 4.4 RSASSA-PSS verification operation (according to [100])
Input: signer's RSA public key (n, e), message M, signature s to be verified
Output: *"signature is valid"* or *"signature is invalid"*
1: $m := s^e \mod n$
2: apply *PSS verification* (Figure 4.4): $result := \text{PSS}_{\text{Verify}}(M, m)$
3: **if** $result = consistent$ **then**
4:    **return** *"signature is valid"*
5: **else**
6:    **return** *"signature is invalid"*
7: **end if**
---

best known attack is *Pollard's rho algorithm*, which is described in [39]. In this work ECC is realized according to the standard in [42, 43]. For more thorough introductions, see [39, 13].

To utilize ECC, the communication partners have to decide on an elliptic curve on which, in turn, the keys are defined and the operations are executed. In the following, such a curve is defined by a parameter set written as a tuple (q, a, b, G, n, h). q is a large prime number and modulus of the finite field $\mathbb{GF}(q)$. a, b are the Weierstraß-coefficients. The generator point of the elliptic curve group is given a $G = (x_G, y_G)$. The order of G is provided as n, which should be a large prime with a size similar to q. h, finally, is the cofactor with $h = \#E/n$.

Note that in this work a is always set to $q - 3$ for ECC. As mentioned in Section 3.3.2, this allows an optimization for the elliptic curve doubling. This does not limit security and the parameter sets used in the prototype also exhibit this property, see Section 7.1. In spite of this, a is included in the domain parameters, because the scheme algorithms depicted below also work for the general case.

To generate a key pair, an integer $x \in [0, n-1]$ is randomly chosen. This number is also the private key. The public key is computed as $Q = xG$. In contrast to RSA, there are no basic en-/decryption operations.

ECIES

The *Elliptic Curve Integrated Encryption Scheme* is taken from [43, 39] and may be used to encrypt a message M. It is special in the way that it actually is a hybrid scheme utilizing both asymmetric and symmetric cryptography. The elliptic curve operations are used to derive a temporary key, which, in turn, is used to en-/decrypt the message with a symmetric algorithm. In this work, AES with counter-mode is exploited as this symmetric algorithm, see Section 4.4.2.

In the algorithms for ECIES, auxiliary functions are utilized. The function $\text{MAC}_k(\cdot)$ denotes a *Message Authentication Code* as described in Section 4.4.5, where k is used as key. The functions $\text{Enc}_k(\cdot)$ and $\text{Dec}_k(\cdot)$ refer to the symmetric encryption and decryption with the key k, respectively. $\text{KDF}(\cdot)$, finally, is a *Key Derivation Function*, which derives

4.1. Public key cryptography

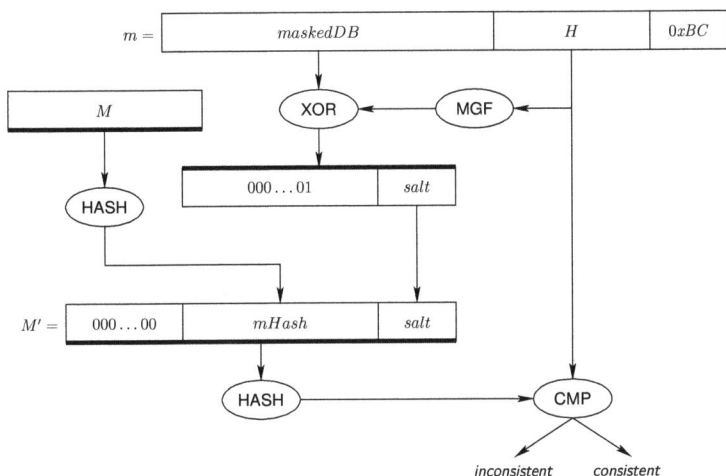

Figure 4.4.: Outline of the PSS verification (from [100])

two temporary keys[3] form a bit string input. In case of ECIES, the coordinates of V and the coordinate x_T are interpreted as bit strings and concatenated to be utilized as this input string. Internally, a MGF is exploited to compute the desired keys, see [43, page 79]. The derived key k_1 is utilized in the symmetric encryption, while the key k_2 is used for the computation of the MAC.

The encryption according to the ECIES is shown in pseudo-code in Algorithm 4.5. It encrypts a message m with the public key Q into the ciphertext (V, c, t).

Algorithm 4.5 ECIES encryption algorithm (according to [39])

Input: domain parameters (q, a, b, G, n, h), public key $Q \in E$, message M
Output: ciphertext (V, c, t)
1: select $u \in [1, n-1]$ randomly
2: $V := uG$
3: $T := uQ = (x_T, y_T)$; **if** $T = \mathcal{O}$ **then** go to step 1
4: $(k_1, k_2) := \text{KDF}(x_T, V)$
5: $c := \text{Enc}_{k_1}(M)$
6: $t := \text{MAC}_{k_2}(c)$
7: **return** (V, c, t)

Its counterpart, i.e., the decryption is shown in Algorithm 4.6. It decrypts the ciphertext (V, c, t) with the private key x and regains the original message M.

---
[3]Actually, just one bit string is returned, which is then split into two parts interpreted as keys.

Chapter 4. Cryptographic aspects

Algorithm 4.6 ECIES decryption algorithm (according to [39])
Input: domain parameters (q, a, b, G, n, h), private key $x \in [0, n-1]$, ciphertext (V, c, t)
Output: message M
1: $T = xR = (x_T, y_T)$
2: **if** $T = \mathcal{O}$ **then return** *reject ciphertext*
3: $(k_1, k_2) := \text{KDF}(x_T, V)$
4: $t' := \text{MAC}_{k_2}(c)$
5: **if** $t' \neq t$ **then return** *reject ciphertext*
6: $M := \text{Dec}_{k_1}(c)$
7: **return** M

ECDSA

The *Elliptic Curve Digital Signature Algorithm* is taken from [42] and allows the generation and verification of signatures. It is based on the *Digital Signature Algorithm* (DSA), which operates on modular numbers. These are substituted by their elliptic curve counterparts leading to an elliptic curve variant of DSA.

The signature operation is depicted in Algorithm 4.7 and results in a signature for the message M, which is a tuple consisting of two integers (c, d). The operation Hash($\cdot$) denotes a hash function as described in Section 4.4.3.

Algorithm 4.7 ECDSA signature algorithm (according to [39])
Input: domain parameters (q, a, b, G, n, h), private key $x \in [0, n-1]$, message M
Output: signature (c, d) with $c, d \in [0, n-1]$
1: select $u \in [1, n-1]$ randomly
2: $V := uG = (x_V, y_V)$
3: $c := x_V \mod n$; **if** c = 0 **then** go to step 1
4: $f := \text{Hash}(M)$
5: $d := u^{-1} \cdot (f + x \cdot c) \mod n$; **if** d = 0 **then** go to step 1
6: **return** (c, d)

The verification operation is shown in Algorithm 4.8. It verifies, whether the signature (c, d) is valid for the message M.

4.1. Public key cryptography

Algorithm 4.8 ECDSA verification algorithm (according to [39])

Input: domain parameters (q, a, b, G, n, h), public key $Q \in E$, signature (c, d) with $c, d \in [0, n-1]$, message M
Output: *"signature is valid"* or *"signature is invalid"*
1: **if** $c \notin [1, n-1]$ or $d \notin [1, n-1]$ **then**
2:    **return** *"signature is invalid"*
3: **end if**
4: $f := \text{Hash}(M)$
5: $h := d^{-1} \mod n$
6: $h_1 := f \cdot h \mod n$
7: $h_2 := c \cdot h \mod n$
8: $P := h_1 G + h_2 Q = (x_P, y_P)$
9: **if** $P = \mathcal{O}$ **then**
10:    **return** *"signature is invalid"*
11: **end if**
12: $c' := x_P \mod n$
13: **if** $c' = c$ **then**
14:    **return** *"signature is valid"*
15: **else**
16:    **return** *"signature is invalid"*
17: **end if**

4.1.3. Pairing-based cryptography

Notation for PBC

q	prime number; size and modulus of $\mathbb{GF}(q)$; $q \equiv 3 \mod 4$
a, b	coefficients of the Weierstraß equation; $a, b \in \mathbb{GF}(q)$
G	generator point generating a subgroup with order n; $G \in E(\mathbb{GF}(q))$
$E(\mathbb{GF}(q))$	elliptic curve over $\mathbb{GF}(q)$
$\#E(\mathbb{GF}(q))$	order of the curve $E(\mathbb{GF}(q))$; $\#E(\mathbb{GF}(q)) = q + 1$
n	prime divisor of $\#E(\mathbb{GF}(q))$ and order of G
h	cofactor to n; $h = \#E(\mathbb{GF}(q))/n$
$E(\mathbb{GF}(q^2))$	elliptic curve over $\mathbb{GF}(q^2)$
$\#E(\mathbb{GF}(q^2))$	order of the curve $E(\mathbb{GF}(q^2))$; $\#E(\mathbb{GF}(q^2)) = (q+1)^2$
x	private key; integer with $x \in [0, n-1]$
Q	public key; point on $E(\mathbb{GF}(q))$ with $Q = xG$
M	message; bit string of arbitrary length
S	signature; point on $E(\mathbb{GF}(q))$

Pairing-based cryptography (PBC) is a relatively new, but lively research area in cryptography. The pairings are used to create new schemes exhibiting different advantages compared to previous approaches. For example, the identity-based schemes promise a simplification of the key management, as it allows to derive the key from some unique

Chapter 4. Cryptographic aspects

identifier like an email-address. For a survey concerning PBC schemes, see [30].

An advantage of PBC is that it does not need a completely new mathematical foundation, but is partly based on the well-researched elliptic curves. Thus, the mathematical foundation is relatively well understood, which promises a relatively high confidence in the security of the developed schemes. Because the research on PBC is relatively new, there exist no standards for schemes yet. Thus, the scheme realized in the prototype is based upon the description in the research publication, see below.

In this work PBC is only intended as proof-of-concept. Thus, only a simple case based on curves with the Weierstraß-equation $y^2 = x^3 + x$ according to [13, page 203] is considered with the security level of just 80 bit. The needed bit-lengths for the modular operations may be deduced from the conditions in [13, page 203]. It states that for a security level of 80 bit it must hold that $n > 2^{160}$ and $q^k > 2^{1024}$. Thus, the size of n is similar to the size of the bit length of ECC and the size of q^k is similar to the size of the bit length of RSA. Because $k = 2$ in this work, q should have a bit length of 512.

BLS Short Signature Scheme

The *BLS Short Signature Scheme* from [16] allows short signatures compared to RSA or ECDSA[4]. However, its verification routine is somewhat expensive, because it needs two pairing computations. The security of the BLS scheme relies, similarly to the ECC schemes, on the *elliptic curve discrete logarithm problem*.

Key Generation Choose a random integer $x \in [0, n-1]$ as private key. Then, the public key Q is calculated as $Q = xG$, where G is the generator point of the elliptic curve.

Signing Given a message M and the private key x, compute $S = x \cdot \text{HashToPoint}(M)$, where $\text{HashToPoint}(M)$ is a hash function, which hashes the message M of arbitrary length to a point on the elliptic curve $E(\mathbb{GF}(q))$, see Section 4.4.6. This is depicted in Algorithm 4.9.

Algorithm 4.9 BLS signature algorithm

Input: domain parameters (q, a, b, G, n, h), private key $x \in [0, n-1]$, message M
Output: signature $S \in E(\mathbb{GF}(q))$
1: $H := \text{HashToPoint}(M)$
2: $S := xH$
3: **return** S

Verification Given a message M, a signature S, and a pairing operation $e(\cdot, \cdot)$, check whether $e(S, G) = e(\text{HashToPoint}(M), Q)$. If both pairings return the same result, the signature is valid, else it is invalid. The verification operation is shown in Algorithm 4.10.

---
[4]Note that it is sufficient to store and transfer the x-coordinate of the signature S, see [16].

Algorithm 4.10 BLS verification algorithm
Input: domain parameters (q, a, b, G, n, h), public key $Q \in E(\mathbb{GF}(q))$, signature $S \in E(\mathbb{GF}(q))$, message M
Output: *"signature is valid"* or *"signature is invalid"*
1: $H := \text{HashToPoint}(M)$
2: $t_1 := e(S, G)$
3: $t_2 := e(H, Q)$
4: **if** $t_1 = t_2$ **then**
5:   **return** *"signature is valid"*
6: **else**
7:   **return** *"signature is invalid"*
8: **end if**

4.2. Abstraction levels

Figure 4.5 shows a classification of above public key approaches into different abstraction levels. It is taken from [60] and extended by PBC. All three considered public key systems share properties and build upon similar operations. Thus, they may be classified into the same abstraction levels. However, ECC and PBC share some parts not needed for RSA. PBC, in turn, exhibits properties not present in RSA and ECC.

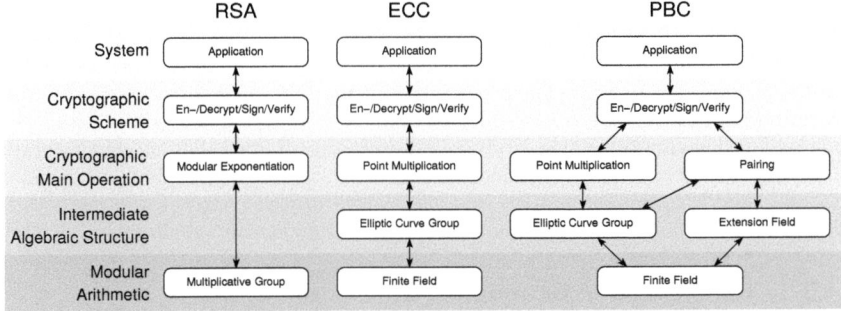

Figure 4.5.: Abstraction levels for different public key algorithms

The *modular arithmetic* is the lowest abstraction level for all three approaches. It contains modular operations like addition, subtraction, and multiplication, which are then utilized by the algorithms on higher abstraction levels. For ECC and PBC the modular arithmetic must be a finite field, i.e., in this work $\mathbb{GF}(q)$, where the modulus q is a prime number. For RSA the modulus n is not a prime, but the product of the large primes p and q, see Section 4.1.1. Thus, the modular arithmetic for RSA is not a finite field, but just a multiplicative group.

The second abstraction level exists only for ECC and PBC and comprises operations in the *intermediate algebraic structures*. For ECC, this is just the *elliptic curve group*,

Chapter 4. Cryptographic aspects

which offers operations to add and double points on an elliptic curve. For PBC there also exists the *extension field*, thus, operations like addition or multiplication in this field are also needed.

The next abstraction level is the *cryptographic main operation*. For RSA, this is the *modular exponentiation*, which builds directly on the modular arithmetic using its properties as a multiplicative group. For ECC and PBC, the *point multiplication* uses the additive group properties of the elliptic curve group. The *pairing*, finally, is part of this abstraction level just for PBC and uses operations of the elliptic curve group and of the extension field.

On the fourth abstraction level a complete *cryptographic scheme* is formed by merging the cryptographic main operation(s) with some cryptographic auxiliary functions like hash function and/or random number generation. For simplicity the auxiliary functions are not shown in Figure 4.5. On the *system* level, finally, the cryptographic schemes are used for some meaningful application.

4.3. Parallelization for public key cryptography

In today's hardware, parallelization is an important approach to improve performance, especially because the amount of available resources still follows Moore's law – doubling every 18 month – but the increase in typical cycles frequencies is declining. Furthermore, doubling the performance by doubling the resources is less power-consuming than by doubling the cycle frequency.

In the following several parallelization techniques for public key algorithms proposed in literature are explained. The presentation of the different approaches is structured according to the abstraction levels introduced above. Note that the parallelization techniques for different abstraction levels do not exclude each other, but an implementation may exploit several of them, as done in this work. Another example for this may be found in the RSA implementation from [86], which utilizes parallelization on both the levels of the modular arithmetic and of the cryptographic main operation.

4.3.1. Parallelization on modular arithmetic level

Hardware modules for modular arithmetic are build up from elementary computational units, which operate on bits or words. To decrease the execution time, multiple instances of these units can be employed in parallel. Because the modular multiplication is the most time consuming operation, there are many proposals to speed it up with parallelization. Parallelizing the remaining modular operations is usually not effective, because those are less time-critical. However, some parallel architectures for the multiplication also require parallelization for the other operations, e.g., buses of full bit-width, see below. Note that the following methods do not form an exhaustive list and do not exclude each other.

Buses of full bit-width In general, the complexity of the multiplication is quadratic with respect to the calculated bit-width. This may be reduced to a merely linear

4.3. Parallelization for public key cryptography

complexity, if all bits are considered at once. This approach, of course, results in a proportional increase of the required resources. An example may be found in [93], where the systolic array used to compute a modular multiplication needs about twice the resources, if the bit-width is doubled. Further implementations with buses of full bit-width may be found for example in [97, 9, 87, 90].

The utilization of buses of full bit-width has as main advantage the linear speed-up, which comes at relatively low costs, because only a small amount of control logic has to be parallelized as well. However, this approach exhibits a certain inflexibility regarding the bit-widths range it may compute. If the current bit-width is smaller than the maximum, resource stay unused. The operation on larger bit-widths than the maximum is not easily possible. The design from [26] solves these problems to some degree by building up an RSA-core with a large bit-width from several ECC-cores with a smaller bit-width each. This solution, however, does not completely avoid above problems, as it still leads to unused resources, if the current bit-width is different from the bit-width of a single ECC-core or multiples of it.

On FPGAs, where the size and structure of the memory is subject to some limitations, buses of full bit-width exhibit a further drawback. To obtain a memory featuring a data bus with sufficient width, several memory blocks have to be utilized in parallel. This often results in a memory size larger than needed for the cryptographic calculations. Although memory realized in the logic cell of the FPGA is more flexible regarding its size and structure, it is usually a poor solution, because the required logic cells are then not available for other tasks.

Pipelining Pipelining may be viewed as counterpart to buses of full bit-width, as it also allows a trade-off between execution time and resource usage. But with this approach the input and output buses may have a width of just one bit or one word.

Most propositions for pipelining build upon the Montgomery multiplication, which allows two possible pipelining strategies.

- As proposed in [118], one pipeline stage is assigned to each step of the inner loop. Because the first step is more complicated than the following steps, this allows the stages except the first one to be kept relatively simple. However, one usually has to employ at least as many stages as the operands have words, because of a data feedback in the algorithm. This also results in unused pipeline stages and, thus, unused resources, if the bit-width is smaller than the maximum.

- [114] presents a more flexible design, which allows the utilization of an arbitrary number of stages and, therefore, a more fine-grained trade-off between execution time and resource usage. This is achieved by assigning one pipeline stage to each step of the outer loop. This keeps the data feedback within a single stage. However, using this approach, each stage must compute all steps of the inner loop including the more complicated first step. Thus, all

Chapter 4. Cryptographic aspects

stages have to be as complex as the first, although the additional resources are needed only seldom.

Residue number systems Residue number systems (RNS) are a somewhat unorthodox approach, as the values are not represented in the μ-radix representation. Rather values are represented relative to a base consisting of several prime moduli, which are prime to each other. If $\{m_1, m_2, \ldots, m_n\}$ is such a base, then for every $a \in [0, M-1]$, where $M = \prod_{i=1}^{n} m_i$, there exists an unique representation consisting of n smaller integers $a_i = a \mod m_i$. Thus, using the abbreviation $x \mod m_i = \langle x \rangle_{m_i}$, an integer a may be written

$$a \Rightarrow \langle a \rangle_M = (\langle a \rangle_{m_1}, \langle a \rangle_{m_2}, \langle a \rangle_{m_3}, \ldots, \langle a \rangle_{m_n}).$$

The existence of the unique mapping between both representations is ensured by the Chinese Remainder Theorem. The representation in an RNS has the advantage that it is possible to calculate the addition, subtraction, and multiplication operations on the residue level. Therefore, as depicted in following equations, these three operations may be parallelized on up to n arithmetical units.

$$\langle a \pm b \rangle_M = (\langle a_1 \pm b_1 \rangle_{m_1}, \langle a_2 \pm b_2 \rangle_{m_2}, \langle a_3 \pm b_3 \rangle_{m_3}, \ldots, \langle a_n \pm b_n \rangle_{m_n})$$
$$\langle a \cdot b \rangle_M = (\langle a_1 \cdot b_1 \rangle_{m_1}, \langle a_2 \cdot b_2 \rangle_{m_2}, \langle a_3 \cdot b_3 \rangle_{m_3}, \ldots, \langle a_n \cdot b_n \rangle_{m_n})$$

Note that these operations are implicitly calculated modulo M.

A drawback of RNS is that comparison and, therefore, division/reduction can not be easily calculated in the RNS representation. Fortunately, this constitutes no real disadvantage for public key algorithms, because the Montgomery multiplication allows to substitute the reduction by a multiplication with the inverse. A detailed description of the mathematical foundations is beyond the scope of this work, but may be found in [4]. Furthermore, several hardware implementations for this approach exist, see for example [20, 107].

4.3.2. Parallelization on intermediate algebraic structure level

Parallelization on this level concerns mainly point addition and doubling, but also operations in the extension field. All of these may be accelerated by executing the modular operations they consist of in parallel. This acceleration, however, is limited by the data dependencies within the algorithms. Note that the algorithms on this level are independent of the bit-widths. Thus, parallelization on this level does not lead to the problems of the modular arithmetic level, namely, resource utilization for different bit-widths and the inflexibility concerning the bit-widths.

There exist several proposals concerning the parallelization of point addition and doubling. This is not the case for the operations in the extension field, because, firstly, the research area is relatively new and, secondly, these operations are relatively simple and straight forward. In literature, see [104, 1], the exploitation of 2 or 3 parallel multiplier instances is usually proposed for realizations of point addition and doubling. Beyond this number, the increased resource requirements can not be justified by the speed-up anymore.

An interesting way of handling the point operations is proposed in [34], as it combines point addition and doubling into a single atomic operation. The resulting algorithm contains more modular multiplications than each point addition and doubling alone. Therefore, more parallel modular instances may be used, while still providing a significant benefit, see [60]. Furthermore, the atomic operation consists of only 19 modular multiplications. This is less than point addition and doubling together, which exhibit 16 and 10 modular multiplications, respectively. As reason for this is that some intermediate results have to be computed only once in the atomic variant.

Finally, this abstraction level is well-suited for parallelization in realizations using hardware supporting SIMD[5], see [1, 47]. This is because this architecture may only execute identical operations in parallel, thus, making parallelization on the level of the modular arithmetic difficult.

4.3.3. Parallelization on cryptographic main operation level

This abstraction level contains modular exponentiation and point multiplication on the one hand and the pairing on the other hand. This division is useful, as former two use only their respective underlying group, i.e., the modular arithmetic and the elliptic points, respectively. Besides this difference, both operations are very similar and may be parallelized by analog approaches.

Using the Montgomery Powering Ladder, two parallel instances of the group operation may by exploited, see [50]. It is depicted as modular exponentiation in Algorithm 4.11, but may be used for the point multiplication as well, as motivated in Section 3.3.3. As described in Chapter 7 it is used for these two operations in this work.

If precomputation may be exploited, [65] proposes a very effective approach reducing the complexity of a modular exponentiation, thus, allowing a trade-off between memory usage and execution time. This may also be used to parallelize a modular exponentiation or a point multiplication. For this, every parallel hardware instance is initialized with one (or more) precomputed value(s) and calculates an intermediate result using a part of the exponent or scalar, respectively. These intermediate results are then combined together in a final calculation leading to the final result.

Because in most schemes the exponent or scalar, respectively, must stay secret, parallelization on this level is often proposed as counter measure against side channel attacks (SCA). The parallel execution of both group operations helps to make the computation time independent from the private key, see [50] ([45] for SIMD). In [78] the point addition and doubling is split into pipeline stages, which allows a partly overlapping calculation of two consecutive operations. Besides a possible speed-up, this also grants better resistance to SCA.

For PBC this abstraction level also includes the pairing. The most common approach

---

[5]Single Instruction, Multiple Data

Chapter 4. Cryptographic aspects

Algorithm 4.11 Montgomery Powering Ladder (from [50])
Input: modulus $m = (m_{n-1}m_{n-2}\ldots m_0)$, base $g < m$, exponent $e \geq 1$ in binary representation with bit-length l (i.e., $e = (e_{l-1}e_{l-2}\ldots e_1 e_0)$)
Output: result $g^e \mod m$
 1: $a := 1, b := 1$
 2: **for** $j = l - 1$ down to 0 **do**
 3:    **if** $e_j = 0$ **then**
 4:       $b := a \cdot b$
 5:       $a := a^2$
 6:    **else**
 7:       $a := a \cdot b$
 8:       $b := b^2$
 9:    **end if**
10: **end for**
11: **return** a

---

for its calculation is Miller's algorithm, whose fundamental buildup follows the point multiplication including several additional operations. Therefore, Miller's algorithm may be parallelized with the same techniques possible for the point multiplication, e.g., the Montgomery Powering Ladder. However, parallelization does not aid resistance against SCA, because the order of the group, which is publicly known, is utilized as "scalar" of the algorithm.

4.3.4. Cryptographic scheme and system levels

These two abstraction levels are addressed mainly because of completeness. Parallelization on these two levels is done only seldom, because it offers smaller improvements than parallelization on lower levels, as the amount of control logic, which has to be parallelized as well, is higher. It is still used in this work, because beyond a certain threshold an increased parallelization on lower levels does not grant a matching acceleration. This is described in detail in Section 6.1.

4.4. Auxiliary cryptographic functions

Within the different cryptographic schemes described in Section 4.1, the auxiliary cryptographic functions *symmetric en-/decryption*, *hash function*, and *Cryptographically Secure Random Number Generator* (CSRNG) are employed. However, their execution time constitutes only a small part of the overall execution time of such a scheme, thus, the resource usage of the auxiliary functions should be kept small, too. In this work, this was done by instantiating each auxiliary function only once and sharing it between the parallel public cryptography scheme modules.

As motivated in Section 6.3 the algorithms for the auxiliary functions are based on

4.4. Auxiliary cryptographic functions

a block cipher as core operation, which further decreases their resource usage. This allows to reuse the resources for the block cipher and makes only a relatively small auxiliary module for each function necessary. In the following, a short introduction to the Advanced Encryption Standard and the algorithms used to implement the auxiliary functions is given. This also includes a Message Authentication Code and a Hash-to-point operation, which both use the other auxiliary functions as building blocks.

4.4.1. Advanced Encryption Standard

The *Advanced Encryption Standard* (AES), see [83], is based on the block cipher Rijndael from [27] and specifies it with the key-lengths 128, 192, and 256 bit and a block length of 128 bit. The encryption operation updates an internal state in several rounds, whose number depends on the key-length. The final state is then put out as result. Each round consists of the four transformations *SubBytes*, *ShiftRows*, *MixColumn*, and *AddRoundKey* in this order. *SubBytes* substitutes the value of each byte of the internal state with a value gained from a look-up table called *S-Box*. *ShiftRows* rotates the four 32-bit rows, in which the state is represented, by different amounts of bytes. *MixColumns* updates each of the columns using a matrix multiplication with a predefined matrix from [83]. *AddRoundKey*, finally, XORes the internal state with the current round key, which is generated based on the secret key.

The decryption contains, basically, the inverse operations executed in reverse order. This is complicated by the fact that round keys are also needed in reverse order. Therefore, they must be calculated in advance, thus, making the decryption operation more costly than the encryption. In this work, however, this is taken into account by utilizing the counter-mode encryption, which executes both encryption and decryption using the encryption operation of the block cipher.

4.4.2. Counter-mode encryption

A block cipher alone encrypts the same plaintext always into the same ciphertext. Thus, if an attacker knows at least some pairs of plain- and ciphertexts, he could generate a dictionary, which could be used on other ciphertexts. Thus, usually a *cryptographic mode* is utilized, in which the block cipher is embedded. As suggested in [66], this work exploits the *counter-mode* to realize symmetric encryption with AES as block cipher.

The approach of the counter-mode is illustrated in Figure 4.6. At first, a sequence of numbers is generated, beginning with a *nonce*[6] and continued with values each time increased by 1.

This sequence is put into the block cipher and the blocks C_i of the ciphertext are obtained by XORing the blocks of the resulting output bit stream with the blocks M_i of the message. Because the XOR operation is its own inversion, the decryption uses the

---

[6]The nonce is an often randomly chosen number, which makes the current en-/decryption unique. Otherwise the same plaintext would always be encrypted into the same ciphertext. Note that because of this, a nonce must not be reused for a different en-/decryption of the same plaintext.

same operations with M and C exchanged. Therefore, the counter-mode exhibits a relatively low resource usage, as it features a general simplicity and because the decryption functionality of the block cipher may be omitted.

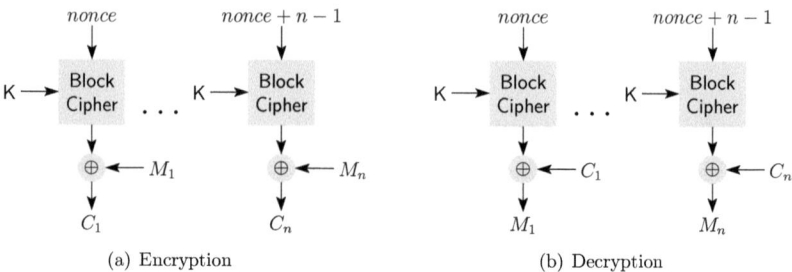

Figure 4.6.: Illustration of en-/decryption in counter-mode

4.4.3. Hash function

A cryptographic *hash function* is an *one-way* function, which may be used to indicate the uniqueness of a message by providing a "fingerprint". In particular, the cryptographic schemes for signature and verification make use of them. A general hash function $H = \text{Hash}(M)$ takes a bit string M of arbitrary length as message and outputs the hash value H of fixed length. A cryptographic hash function additionally needs to have the one-way property, see [108], which may be expressed as follows.

- If the message M is known, the hash value H is easy to compute.
- If the hash value H is known, it is computational infeasible to compute an M with $\text{Hash}(M) = H$.
- If the message M is known, it is computational infeasible to find another message M' with $\text{Hash}(M) = \text{Hash}(M')$.

For use in digital signature generation, *collision resistance* is necessary in addition to the one-way property. Otherwise, it would be possible to find some pair of messages M and M' with $\text{Hash}(M) = \text{Hash}(M')$. This is known as *birthday attack*, because it is similar to finding two persons with the same birthday in a given group. For finding a message by brute-force to a given hash value H, one has to compute 2^n random messages on average. But for finding two messages with the same hash value the calculation of $2^{\frac{n}{2}}$ random messages is sufficient on average. This, essentially, halves the effective security bit length: If one needs 128 bits for security (probability of 1 in 2^{128}), a hash function with an output length of 256 bits is needed.

To implement a hash function based upon a block cipher, the *Davies-Meyer* method described in [71] may be used. This is proposed in [23] employing AES. However, AES in its standardized form features only a block length of 128 bit, which would lead to 128 bit as output length of the hash function. This is too short, because of security reasons, see above. Thus, in [23] the general Rijndael block cipher[7] from [27] is used, where both key and block length were set to 256 bit.

Following [23], the input stream is divided into n blocks $x_1, x_2, \ldots, x_n$ with a length of 256 bit each. Subsequently, the hash value H is calculated according to

$$H_0 = 2^{256} - 1 \tag{4.1a}$$
$$H_i = \text{Enc}_{x_i}(H_{i-1}) \oplus H_{i-1}, \quad 0 < i \leq n \tag{4.1b}$$
$$H = H_{n+1} = \text{Enc}_{H_n}(H_n) \oplus H_n, \tag{4.1c}$$

where $\text{Enc}_a(b)$ denotes the encryption of b with the key a using the block cipher.

4.4.4. Cryptographically secure random number generator

Compared to general random number generators, the output of a *Cryptographically Secure Random Number Generator* (CSRNG) has to feature a higher quality. Otherwise, attackers could guess random bits and use certain statistical approaches to reduce the amount of possible secret keys. This may be expressed by two properties, see [108]:

1. The output of a CSRNG must look *random*, i.e., it must be impossible to distinguish it from an actual random stream.

2. The output must be *unpredictable*, i.e., it must be computational infeasible to predict the next bit, even if the algorithm and the previous bits are known.

Thus, designing a new algorithm demands extensive examinations. This may be avoided by employing a standardized algorithm for the implementation of a CSRNG. [6] proposes a method utilizing a block cipher as core element. In this work, this was used to implement a CSRNG based upon the AES core, which allowed to reuse these resources.

According to [6], an important element of the RNG is its internal state, which consists of an internal key and a value V. In each operation the state is updated, i.e., substituted by new values. These new values and the generated random bits are computed based on the old state using the block cipher. The state needs to be initialized and periodically reinitialized using some seed numbers.

4.4.5. Message Authentication Code

A *Message Authentication Code* (MAC) is an one-way hash function, which also depends on a secret key. Thus, the hash value can only be verified by owners of this key. This can be used to authenticate messages between users of a group without providing secrecy. A simple way to implement a MAC function is to encrypt the hash-value with a symmetric algorithm.

---

[7]Note that in this work the term AES is used, although it may be Rijndael in a strict sense.

Chapter 4. Cryptographic aspects

In the prototype implementation for the co-processor the *keyed-Hash Message Authentication Code* (HMAC) from [84] is used. An HMAC is a MAC, which is calculated based on a hash function. This simplifies the creation of new MACs featuring high confidence in their security, because of the trust in the underlying hash function. Furthermore, this may also allow reuse of the code for the hash function.

4.4.6. Hash-to-point

The *Hash-to-point* operation is similar to the normal hash function, but maps a message to a point on the elliptic curve and not to an integer value. This is needed in the pairing-based scheme described in Section 4.1.3.

Internally, the Hash-to-point operation first uses a standard hash function to map the message M to an integer value $H := \text{Hash}(M)$, which is then uniquely mapped to a point P on the elliptic curve E. This unique mapping is realized in two consecutive steps:

1. The integer $H := \text{Hash}(M)$ is interpreted as coordinate x'_P of a point $P' = (x'_P, y'_P)$, for which a suitable coordinate y'_P is needed. Because the *Weierstraß*-equation for the pairing-based cryptography in this work is $y^2 = x^3 + x$, this may be done by calculating $y'_P = \sqrt{H^3 + H} \mod q$. Note that this square root may not exist, in which case a different point must be found deterministically. According to [109], this can by done by choosing $P' = (-H, \sqrt{-H^3 - H} \mod q)$ instead.

2. Although the point P' is on the elliptic curve E, it is not necessarily a part of the cyclic subgroup of E used in the cryptographic computations. Therefore, P' is multiplied with the cofactor h resulting in a point $P = hP'$, which is part of the cyclic subgroup of E.

Chapter 5.
Hardware platform

The prototype implementation introduced in this work was realized on an FPGA development board, which is described in this chapter. FPGAs contain many elementary hardware components, whose connection can be changed allowing the "(re)programming" of arbitrary circuitry. The Boolean logic and the registers are realized by a large amount of basic configurable logic blocks distributed over the whole device. Today's FPGAs usually also provide more specialized components for tasks the basic blocks are not so well-suited for, e.g., memory, arithmetical operations, or input/output. The connections between the components are established using a wire-grid called routing resources.

FPGAs are useful for applications neither pure software or pure hardware solutions are well-suited for. Compared to pure hardware implementations like ASICs[1], FPGAs are slow. However, the development of applications for FPGAs is cheaper, because their programming and debugging is easier. Thus, FPGAs are usually used instead of ASICs for small batch productions, where the cheaper costs per unit of ASICs can not offset their increased development costs. Compared to pure software realizations, FPGA designs are of course faster, but also more expensive to develop. Thus, FPGAs are usually only used, if the speed of a software implementation is not sufficient. Furthermore, FPGAs are often utilized for prototyping in the design phase of hardware solutions.

The basic design flow for the development of an FPGA realization starts with the description in a *hardware description language* (HDL) like VHDL. With the help of several software tools, this description is translated into a bit stream, which is needed for the actual configuration of the FPGA. In the *synthesis* the Boolean logic is translated into the elementary component types available on the particular FPGA platform. Then, the step *place and route* maps these instantiated components to physical components of the FPGA, i.e., it is decided, which actual existing component is used to implement a particular Boolean function. This step also decides the routing, i.e., how the components are connected via the routing resources. This is of special importance, because it may not be possible to maintain the desired cycle period, if the physical placement of two elements is too far apart. From the description produced by the *place and route*, the bit stream is generated, which may be used to program the FPGA. After loading this bit stream into the FPGA, it finally exhibits the desired functionality. For a more detailed description, see [111, 119].

Thanks to Moore's law, today's FPGAs have reached a size, where it is possible to

---
[1] Application Specific Integrated Circuit

instantiate multiple cores and the buses connecting them on the same device. Because of their reconfigurability allowing the reuse of one physical device for different designs, FPGAs are a relative cheap development platform for *(Multi-processor) System-on-a-Chip* ((MP)SoC) designs. This is also widely exploited in the research of such architectures, as done in this work.

5.1. XUP Virtex-II Pro Development System

The prototype implementation was realized on an XUP^2 *Virtex-II Pro Development System* from Digilent, Inc. This platform is an external board for the development of applications using a Virtex-II Pro FPGA from Xilinx. The board is depicted in Figure 5.1.

The main component of the board is of course the Virtex-II Pro FPGA, which is described below in more detail. Besides this, the board features many components allowing the development of a wide range of applications. For this work, only the following components were utilized: The DDR SDRAM slot was equipped with 256 MByte of RAM and was used as off-chip memory. The communication between FPGA and host system was executed via the RS-232 port. The USB2 port was also needed, but only for loading the bit stream onto the FPGA and the program code for the PowerPC into the off-chip memory.

Furthermore, the board features a 10/100 Ethernet port, a Compact Flash card slot, an XSGA Video port, an Audio Codec, a SATA interface, and PS/2 ports for a mouse and a keyboard. Together with standard PC Hardware, this allows for example the use of *uCLinux*, which is a Linux derivative intended for smaller micro controllers, see [2]. Finally, the board exhibits expansion connectors allowing the attachment of custom expansion boards containing additional ports or hardware.

5.2. Virtex-II Pro FPGA

The FPGA on the XUPV2P board is a Virtex-II Pro (xc2vp30ff896-7), see [123]. It contains as central building block 13,696 *slices*, which are important building blocks for the reconfigurable logic. Furthermore, the FPGA features on-chip memory arranged as block RAM, dedicated word multipliers, 3-state buffers, Digital Clock Managers (DCM) easily allowing different clock domains, and fast IO-ports called RocketIO with a speed of up to 3,125 GBit/s.

Not all of these basic components present in the FPGA were utilized in the prototype implementation. Therefore, only the required components are described in more detail below. On a higher abstraction level the basic components are utilized to form the elements of a SoC architecture, which are explained subsequently.

---

[2]Xilinx University Program

5.2. Virtex-II Pro FPGA

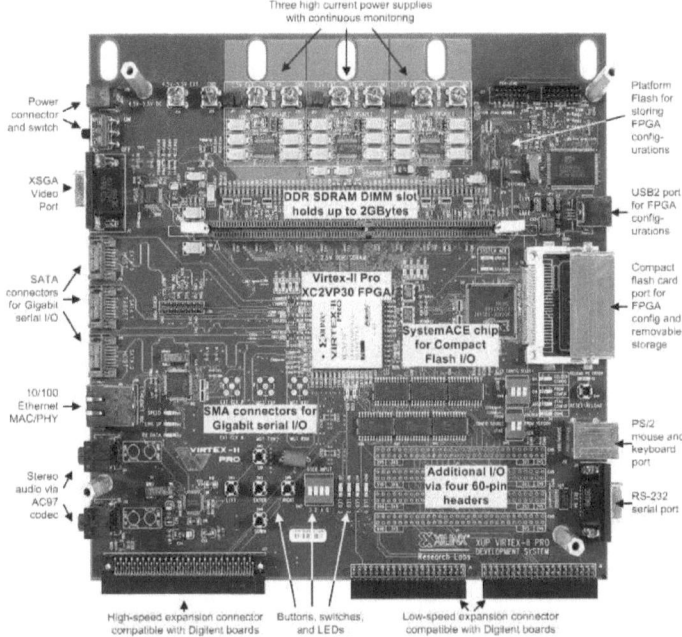

Figure 5.1.: XUP Virtex-II Pro Development System (from [122])

5.2.1. Basic components

The basic components are those components, which are native to the FPGA. Phrased differently, they are available independently from the concrete application. Here, only those components are explained, which are utilized in the prototype implementation.

Slice This is perhaps the most important building block of the reconfigurable logic. Each slice consists mainly of two function generators realized as *Look-up-Table*s (LUT) and two storage elements, which may be used in different ways. Furthermore, it contains several 2:1-multiplexers (MUX) and special arithmetical logic.

Besides their basic application realizing Boolean functions, the LUTs may also be used as distributed RAM and shift registers. If configured as distributed memory, 16 bit of storage with a data bus width of 1 bit can be stored in 1 or 2 LUTs, respectively, depending on whether the memory should be single- or dual-ported. However, note that distributed memory does not allow two truly independent ports, as only one of them may be used for write access. Similarly, each LUT may be configured as shift register with a width of 16 bit.

Each of the storage elements of a slice may be used either as register or as latch,

Chapter 5. Hardware platform

respectively, with a size of 1 bit. The multiplexers may be used to interconnect the LUTs into larger function generators or to form larger multiplexers. The arithmetical logic allows the realization of a 2-bit full-adder in one slice[3]. As each slice also contains special ports for the creation of fast carry-chains, several slices may be configured to compose fast and wide adders.

Finally, the reconfigurable building block on the next abstraction level is the *configurable logic block* (CLB). Each CLB consists of four slices together with two 3-state buffers, see below.

3-state buffer For the realization of on-chip buses, the FPGA contains 3-state buffers with a width of 1 bit. Each 3-state buffer may be controlled independently, because each features its own 3-state control port and its own input port. As described above, a CLB contains two 3-state buffers together with four slices.

Block RAM The Virtex-II Pro features 2,448 Kbit of block RAM (BRAM) arranged in 136 blocks each with a size of 18 Kbit. Each of this blocks may be accessed via two truly independent ports. The access ports can be configured to exhibit different data word sizes ranging from 1 to 36 bit.

Dedicated multiplier The FPGA features 136 dedicated word multipliers. Each multiplier has two inputs with a width of 18 bit each and an output with a width of 36 bit. Thus, it may compute the product of two signed 18-bit numbers or of two unsigned numbers with a width of up to 17 bit each. If both inputs and the output are connected to registers, the multipliers can be used in a pipelined version, computing one multiplication in each clock cycle.

PowerPC core The Virtex-II Pro FPGA contains two embedded PowerPC PPC405 cores. Especially for SoC realizations, this is very advantageous, as it provides a fast general purpose processor, which does not take up resources of the reconfigurable components.

Because of the dedicated word multipliers and the BRAM, which also allows memory access on a word-basis, the prototype implementation is realized on a word-basis. This allows the calculation of numbers with several bits in one clock cycle. Furthermore, the arithmetical logic in the slices together with the carry-chains also allows the creation of word adders.

5.2.2. Derived SoC architecture

The basic components of the FPGA may be used to implement nearly every functionality. For applications, where the FPGA plays the role of a fast computational unit mainly executing data flow operations, e.g., utilized as *digital signal processor* (DSP), it is

---
[3]Note that the arithmetical logic also contains elements to improve the efficiency of multiplier implementations. This is, however, not used in this work, because the dedicated multipliers are utilized instead.

5.2. Virtex-II Pro FPGA

possible to design the circuits in VHDL and to use the conventional design flow. But as mentioned above, today's FPGA are large enough to realize complete (MP)SoC. For the design of such complex systems more powerful design tools with components on higher abstraction levels are needed.

Xilinx also provides such design tools, as described in Section 5.3. With them, it is possible to instantiate an architecture consisting of general purpose processors, their instruction and data storage, and additional pre-configured IP-cores like buses and interfaces. It is even possible to integrate custom hardware cores into this architecture. In the following, the two available processor types and the available bus types are described shortly. For more details and information about other available IP-cores, consult the documentation available on [121].

PowerPC

The Virtex-II Pro FPGA features two PowerPC PPC405 cores. These are powerful general purpose processors also suitable for complex application requiring a full-blown operating system. The PowerPC cores are a 64 bit architecture with a 32 bit subset and may be clocked with up to 300 MHz.

MicroBlaze

The second type of general purpose processor available for the design of SoC is a soft-core processor type called *MicroBlaze*. It is build up from the reconfigurable elements of the FPGA and may be instantiated in customized variants providing different amounts of computing power, e.g., with or without dedicated word multiplication. The MicroBlaze processors support 32 bit operations and may be clocked with up to 100 MHz.

Buses

The Xilinx design environment also provides several bus types allowing the general purpose processors to communicate with the memory, other cores, and/or each other. These are explained in the following.

On-Chip Memory Bus The *On-Chip Memory Bus* (OCM) may be utilized by a PowerPC core to communicate with its instruction or data memory. Each PowerPC core possesses one port for the Data-Side On-Chip Memory Bus (DSOCM) with a width of 32 bit and one port for the Instruction-Side On-Chip Memory Bus (ISOCM) with a width of 64 bit.

Processor Local Bus The *Processor Local Bus* (PLB) is a general bus for the PowerPC cores. Each PowerPC possesses one port to connect to a PLB, which may be used to communicate with other IP-cores or memory attached to the PLB. The PLB has a widths of 64 bit, which, however, is only fully exploited, if the bus is cached. To access components attached to the PLB, the PowerPC uses memory-mapped I/O.

Local Memory Bus The *Local Memory Bus* (LMB) may be utilized by a MicroBlaze core to communicate with its instruction or data memory. Each MicroBlaze core possesses one port for the Instruction Local Memory Bus (ILMB) and one port for the Data Local Memory Bus (DLMB) with a width of 32 bit each allowing to access instruction and data storage, respectively.

Open Processor Bus The *Open Processor Bus* (OPB) is a general bus for the MicroBlaze cores. Each MicroBlaze core possesses one port to connect to an OPB and, thus, to communicate with other IP-cores or memory attached to the OPB. The OPB has a width of 32 bit. The access of components by the MicroBlaze is realized with memory-mapped I/O. Communication between cores attached to a PLB and cores connected to an OPB is possible using a PLB-OPB-bridge.

Fast Simplex Link The *Fast Simplex Link* (FSL) is a relative simple bus for communication between a MicroBlaze core and a custom IP-core. Each MicroBlaze possesses up to 8 FSL ports. This is a powerful tool to realize instruction code extensions. The communication is port-mapped and there are specific processor instructions for the access of the FSL. Those instructions allow the MicroBlaze to write and read 32 bit integers to and from an attached core. The communication may be synchronous or asynchronous, facilitated by a FIFO-queue.

5.3. Design flow

Besides the hardware devices, Xilinx also provides the software tools needed for the development of FPGA designs. The *Integrated Software Environment* (ISE) contains all the tools necessary to develop a design in an HDL and, subsequently, synthesize it. The final result is a bit stream, which can be loaded into the FPGA.

This, however, allows only the realization of systems on a basic hardware level, where the designer is responsible for all cores and their connections. To ease this task for the designer, he may use the *Embedded Development Kit* (EDK) bundle with its central suite *Xilinx Platform Studio* (XPS), see [121]. It allows to easily instantiate IP-components like cores, buses, and memory and to configure their behavior. This way, the hardware architecture for embedded applications may be created easily. The XPS is also able to compile software written by the designer and assign it into the appropriate instruction and/or data storage of an instantiated general purpose processor.

The XPS does also help with the integration of custom hardware cores by providing wizards, which create hardware descriptions for customized bus connections. This way, the designer must only write little additional code connecting the custom core to the customized bus interface.

Chapter 6.
Novel flexible and efficient co-processor architecture for server applications

To support a server in today's increasingly heterogeneous networks, the design of the public key cryptographic co-processor follows two main goals.

- Because the co-processor is aimed at server-based applications, it should be primarily optimized for high throughput. The latency of a single cryptographic scheme calculation has a low priority as long as the delay is not noticeable. However, the latency should still be decreased as long this does not restrict the throughput.

- The co-processor should support different cryptographic schemes to allow the communication with a wide range of different clients. Furthermore, to be able to cope with technology changes, it should be relatively easy to upgrade the supported schemes.

A consequence of the goal to support different cryptographic schemes is a wide range of possible bit-widths for the modular operations. RSA requires computations with relatively large numbers with a lengths of up to several thousand bits, while ECC is based on calculations with numbers of only a few hundred bits. The bit-widths for the numbers operated on in PBC lies somewhere in between these two extremes. In the following the bit-widths range from 160 to 3072 is used as an example, because it is considered in the prototype implementation, see Section 7.1.

Finally, for the execution of the complete schemes some auxiliary functions like hash function and random number generation are needed. Because the cryptographic co-processor shall be realized as a single-chip design to reduce eavesdropping risk, these functions have to be implemented on-chip.

6.1. Architectural decisions

The co-processor is to be geared for high throughput, while low latency of a single scheme execution is not as important. To gain high throughput the available resources have to be exploited as continuously as possible, i.e., the architecture should allow an execution order, which minimizes the amount of unused resources at all times. However, although latency is of secondary importance, it should still be decreased as long as this does not restrict throughput. In combination with high flexibility this leads to the following architectural decisions.

6.1.1. HW/SW co-design

The HW/SW co-design approach allows to combine the goal of continuously used resources with the goal of flexibility. Firstly, the realization of the control flow intensive parts of the different schemes in software supports the flexibility, because software is more suited to this task. Furthermore, the control flow intensive tasks are not time-critical, but often have to wait for the time-critical parts to finish. Therefore, this results only in small costs in terms of execution time, as the data flow intensive parts responsible for the majority of the running time may still be implemented in hardware. Secondly, unused resources are avoided, if control flow intensive parts are implemented in software.

As described in Section 4.2, RSA, ECC, and PBC all build upon similar basic functions, in particular, modular arithmetic. Thus, the modular arithmetic may be supported by a common hardware core shared by the computations of all schemes. The algorithms on higher abstraction levels, however, are quite different. A realization of those algorithms in software generally costs less than a hardware implementation, because both programming and debugging overhead are smaller.

The implementation in software may even lead to an increased throughput: Although there is a small increase in execution time, it allows a better resource reuse, thus, leaving more resources for additional parallel calculation instances. This better resource reuse stems from the fact that an implementation in software consists of a general purpose processor and memory to store the program code. An increase in functionality may be achieved by a memory upgrade to store the additional program code for this new functionality. Thus, except for the increase in memory size, the resource usage stays the same. By comparison, a pure hardware realization requires one finite state machine for each supported scheme. However, only one of these finite state machines is running at each point in time. The remaining state machines – thus, their resources – stay unused.

Note that for few and/or simple schemes, a pure hardware implementation variant could be less costly, if the amount of resources needed for all state machines is less than the amount of resources needed for the processor. However, in the prototype realization this was not the case: One MicroBlaze processor requires about double the resources the finite state machine for the point multiplication alone would need, which does not yet include the functionality for EC schemes or for any RSA or PBC computation at all.

6.1.2. HW/SW partitioning

An important decision for an HW/SW co-design implementation is the so-called HW/SW partitioning. It describes which parts are realized in hardware and which in software. Usually, it is beneficial to execute the data flow intensive parts in hardware, because they bear the major part of the actual calculations. Thus, they are rather time-critical and contain less exceptions complicating the algorithm flow. In contrast, the control flow intensive parts are usually executed in software, which is more suited to handle special cases in the program flow. Also, these parts of the implementation normally contain less calculations and, therefore, do not suffer as much from the speed disadvantage of a software realization.

This division of the different parts is also valid for the co-processor architecture developed in this work. The most data flow intensive part is the modular arithmetic on the lowest abstraction level. The higher levels contain mainly control flow, as they mainly control the order, in which the modular operations are executed. Therefore, the modular operations should be realized in dedicated hardware cores, while the remaining algorithms from all abstraction levels above the modular arithmetic should be implemented in software.

An exception pose the cryptographic auxiliary functions, which are not included in the abstraction level view in Figure 4.5. They are time-critical, but only utilized during a small part of the overall execution time of a single scheme. Thus, they must be fast to prevent them from becoming the bottleneck. However, they should also be compact leaving the majority of resources to the modular arithmetic, which bears the majority of the computational work. These two properties are taken into account by sharing the core from [61] between the different processors executing the cryptographic schemes. This core employs a compact block cipher module as central element, which is shared for the execution of the auxiliary functions, see Section 6.3.

The HW/SW partitioning is shown in Figure 6.1. The cores for modular arithmetic and auxiliary functions are implemented in hardware, while the actual schemes are executed in software together with some functionality providing input/output and main control over the scheme executions.

6.1.3. Modular arithmetic core

The modular operations, in particular the modular multiplications, are time-critical. Thus, the core for the modular arithmetic has to be highly efficient, while avoiding unused resources, which would decrease throughput. The efficiency may be increased by utilizing parallelization to speed-up the calculations. In this context, the main focus is on the multiplication, as the remaining modular operations are much faster to begin with. Note that in this work the computations are executed in a word-based manner, because the FPGA as intended platform is well-suited for this. The basic contemplations are, however, also valid for calculations on bit-basis.

Generally, the fastest implementation for the multiplication module is achieved by optimizing it for operations of a single bit-width only. Then, however, one multiplier instance is required for each supported bit-width and the instances for other bit-widths than that currently needed – i.e., the resources used for them – stay unused. On FPGAs, the reconfigurability may be utilized to load modules optimized for the needed bit-length on demand, thus, avoiding unused resources. Unfortunately, this approach exhibits some drawbacks. Loading a module into the FPGA takes a significant amount of time, during which the concerned parts of the FPGA can not compute anything useful. Furthermore, additional resources are needed for the functionality to load and access different modules. Finally, the size of the different module designs depends on the bit-width. Thus, one

Chapter 6. Novel flexible and efficient co-processor architecture for server applications

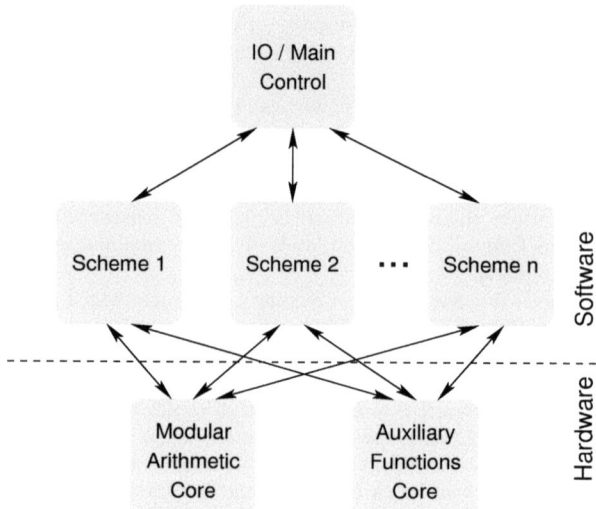

Figure 6.1.: HW/SW partitioning

would have to find a schedule utilizing all FPGA resources at all times.

Instead, to achieve continuously used resources this work proposes to utilize a design, which allows to calculate operations of different bit-widths using the same hardware. For this, the common approach in literature suggests a module optimized for the maximum bit-width, which is also able to operate on shorter bit-widths. This, however, leads to unused resources for calculations with bit-widths smaller than the maximum. The solution from [26] somewhat alleviates this problem by proposing a systolic array with a bit-width suitable for RSA, which is build up from several smaller systolic arrays each featuring a bit-width suitable for ECC. This, however, still leads to unused resources, if the currently calculated bit-width is not a multiple of the shorter bit-length.

Pipelining according to [114] allows a more fine grained trade-off between parallelization degree and usage of resources. It allows an arbitrary amount of pipeline stages and the multiplication module may be optimized for shorter bit-lengths still accelerating longer bit-lengths. As advantage of this approach the resources are utilized relatively evenly for many different bit-lengths. Note that with this pipelining strategy the computed word-count is always a multiple of the amount of stages. Therefore, different numbers of stages lead to different trade-offs between resource usage and acceleration for shorter and longer bit-widths. To minimize unproductive execution time, the number of stages should be as close as possible to factors of all possible bit-lengths, thus, small amounts of stages promise a small overhead for many different word-counts. Unfortunately, this leads to a somewhat low parallelization degree, which may be compensated by also considering parallelization on higher abstraction levels.

6.1.4. Parallelization on higher abstraction levels

On the abstraction level above the modular arithmetic, parallel instances of the modular multiplier may be utilized. As described in Section 4.3.3, RSA is able to exploit two parallel modular multipliers using the Montgomery Powering Ladder. Because RSA – in contrast to the point operations of ECC and PBC, see Section 4.3.2 – is not able to take advantage of a third multiplier instance, only two parallel instances are instantiated in each core for the modular operations. These two multipliers may also be utilized in parallel for the modular exponentiation used for the modular inversion and the modular square root, see Section 3.2.

It would also be feasible to parallelize the cryptographic main operation of ECC and PBC, e.g., by exploiting one instance of point addition and doubling each and applying the Montgomery Powering Ladder. However, the resources necessary for these operations could not be exploited for RSA. Thus, this parallelization is not done in the proposed architecture.

On the level of the cryptographic scheme, finally, parallelization is not restricted, because there are no data dependencies between different scheme executions. Therefore, the only limitation for the degree of parallelization on this level are the available resources needed for the parallel cores computing the cryptographic schemes.

The concrete decisions on the number of pipeline stages and on the number of cores for the scheme execution are left open for now. Additional pipeline stages allow faster computation of modular multiplications and come at a relatively small price in terms of resources. But calculations with smaller bit-widths are not able to take full advantage of too many pipeline stages. Additional cores for the scheme execution, in contrast, double the resource usage, but also double the execution speed for all supported bit-widths.

Thus, different trade-offs between the length of the pipelines – i.e., parallelization degree on the lowest level – and the number of parallel scheme executions – i.e., parallelization degree on the level of the cryptographic scheme – are possible. This is examined in Chapter 8 by experimenting with different variants, which feature different pipeline lengths and resulting numbers of parallel scheme executions.

Note that parallelization using precomputation was completely ignored, because it is not easy to combine the concept of precomputation with the co-processor's flexibility. Additionally, it would have increased the required memory space, which is already in short supply on the used FPGA.

6.1.5. Resulting co-processor architecture

Above considerations result in the proposed co-processor architecture, which is depicted in Figure 6.2. Note that this is a simplified representation abstracting from specifics of a realization. An illustration incorporating concrete implementation details is deferred to Chapter 7.

Chapter 6. Novel flexible and efficient co-processor architecture for server applications

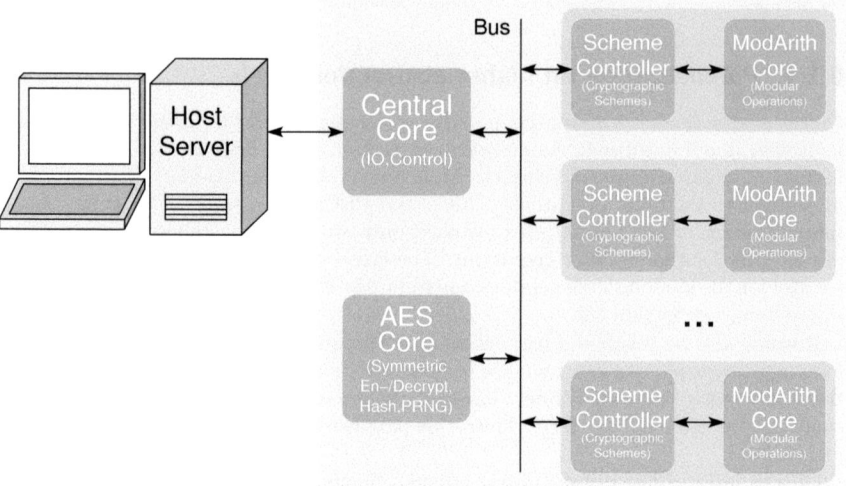

Figure 6.2.: Proposed co-processor architecture

The time-critical modular operations are executed by specialized cores for the modular arithmetic called *ModArith*. They consist of two pipelined modules for modular multiplication and one module for the remaining modular arithmetic. This allows to execute the multiplications in parallel to each other and in parallel to the remaining modular arithmetic. A further parallelization of latter one is not useful, because those operations are already very fast compared to the multiplications. The arrangement of these modules within the ModArith core together with the associated memory architecture is explained in more detail in Section 6.2 and depicted in Figure 6.6.

Each ModArith core is assigned to and controlled by a general purpose processor named *scheme controller*. These processors are responsible for the control flow of the cryptographic schemes present on the higher abstraction levels.

The less important but still time-critical auxiliary functions, namely, symmetric encryption, hash function, and random number generation are provided by an additional core, which is shared by the scheme controllers in a time-multiplex manner. As proposed in Section 6.1.2 the calculation of the auxiliary functions is based on a block cipher module. Because the AES algorithm is utilized for this block cipher, the core for the auxiliary functions is denoted *AES core* in Figure 6.2,

Communication with the *host server* and main control is carried out by a further general purpose processor named *central control*. All cores are connected via a *bus*, which allows communication between them.

Each cryptographic scheme is calculated according to the following basic execution order, which is also depicted in Figure 6.3:

62

1. The host server issues a request to compute a cryptographic scheme operation to the co-processor, which is received by the central core. The request contains the data to en-/decrypt or sign/verify, respectively, and the parameters for the cryptographic scheme, e.g., curve parameters and key pair. Note that parameters for the scheme and the key pair should normally already be stored in the co-processor and only referenced to by the host system. This reduces the eavesdropping risk, because the sensible information, i.e., the private key, does not leave the co-processor.

2. The central core, then, stores the request and dispatches its computation to a scheme controller as soon as one is idle, i.e., not executing another scheme at the moment.

3. Subsequently, the scheme controller starts to calculate the necessary operations for the particular scheme using its own ModArith core (*3a*) and the shared AES core (*3b*).

4. After the completion of the scheme execution, the scheme controller returns the result to the central core and waits for the next command from the central core.

5. Finally, the central core returns the result received from the scheme controller to the host server.

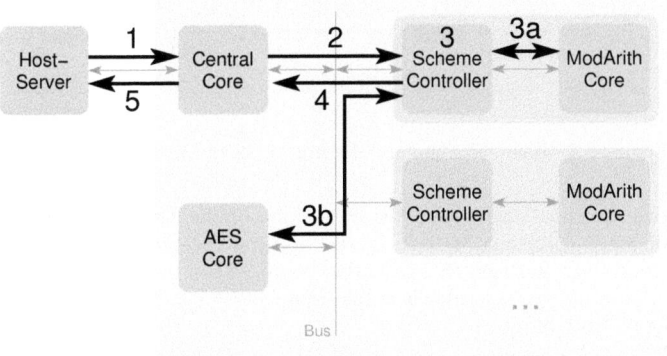

Figure 6.3.: Basic execution order

6.2. Modular arithmetic core

This section presents a more in-depth description of the internals of the ModArith core providing the modular arithmetic. It starts with details on the modular multipliers using short pipelines. This is followed by the presentation of the utilized parallel memory architecture allowing parallel access for multiple multipliers, thus, enabling a continuous execution. At the end, the remaining modular operation besides the multiplication are covered.

6.2.1. Modular multiplication using short pipelines

Because of above described restrictions to parallelization, pipelining according to [114] with only a few stages is employed for the modular multiplication. As described in Section 4.3.1, this pipelining strategy utilizes the Montgomery multiplication and assigns each step of its outer loop, see line 2 to 5 of Algorithm 3.5, to one stage. This allows to use less pipelining stages than the number of words.

Figure 6.4 shows a simplified depiction of the data paths of the pipelined modular multiplier. A variant including the realization specifics is deferred to Chapter 7. The variable names are taken from the description in Algorithm 3.5. The main difference to the design from [114] is the lack of a queue caching the results from the last stage until they are needed again by the first stage. The functionality of this queue is also executed by the *memory* used to store the input values.

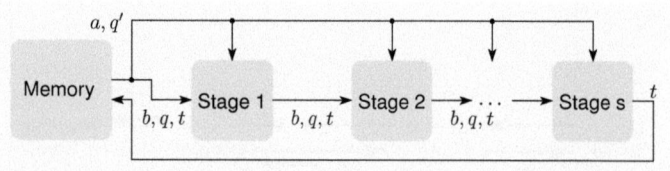

Figure 6.4.: Basic pipeline architecture of the modular multiplication

Each stage executes one step of the outer loop of the Montgomery multiplication. After a stage has completed its calculation, it starts the execution of another step of the outer loop not yet executed by another stage. Thus, *stage 1* computes the steps $i = 0, s, 2s, \ldots$, while *stage 2* calculates the steps $i = 1, s+1, 2s+1, \ldots$, where s denotes the number of available stages.

The words of the variables b, q, t are fed into the first stage, which passes it on to the next stage with the necessary timing delay. This is repeated by the following stages until the values reach the last stage, which writes the words of the intermediate value t back into the memory. The value q' is needed by all stages for their computations, thus, fed to them via a special input port. As the words of the value a are also needed in a different order, they are transferred via these connections, too. Note that because of the memory architecture, see Section 6.2.2, the utilized memory may be accessed each clock cycle with a data-width of just one word. Thus, each execution of one step of the inner loop in one stage takes several cycles needed to read and write the data in addition to the actual calculations.

6.2.2. Parallel memory architecture

Because the computation modules inside the ModArith core must be able to run in parallel, a suitable memory architecture is required. This parallel memory architecture for the modular arithmetic was proposed by the author in [58, 60]. It is intended for FPGAs, scales well with the number of modular multipliers, and allows for low overhead concerning runtime.

Constraints for the memory architecture

By deciding on an FPGA as realization platform, the designer is also restricted to the memory types available on this FPGA. As described in Chapter 5 the Virtex-II Pro offers two kinds of memory: Firstly, the FPGA comprises 136 blocks of dedicated RAM with a size of 16 Kbit[1] each, which is called *Block RAM* (BRAM). Secondly, the slices in the FPGA may be configured as *distributed memory*, which allows a better customization of size and data-width of the memory.

For the proposed co-processor the BRAM is used because of the following reasons. Two BRAMs provide enough storage space for the necessary parameter values. Using distributed memory with an equivalent size would require 2048 slices, which would then not be available for computations. Furthermore, this memory is needed for each ModArith core, which makes the utilization of distributed memory even more prohibitive. Additionally, the modular multiplication exploits pipelining, which does not need buses of full bit-width, but may be done with buses of word-width only. Thus, an especially tailored data bus for the memory, which would make more BRAMs or the utilization of distributed memory necessary, is not required. Finally, as noted in Section 5.2.1, distributed memory, in contrast to BRAM, does not offer two truly independent memory ports, which are needed as described below.

After deciding on the memory type, the constraints for the memory structure have to be examined. As described above, each ModArith core features two parallel multiplier modules and – parallel to the multipliers – one module for the remaining modular arithmetic. For an even resource usage, the memory architecture must allow these modules, in particular the multipliers, to run as continuously as possible. This means that the architecture must be able to continuously feed data into all modules. Otherwise, a module would be stalled in its execution, because the necessary data is not available in time.

Conventional memory architecture

The conventional solution for such a memory architecture is depicted in Figure 6.5: Every module is equipped with input and output registers, which are fed from a single central memory, see [9, 10]. This way, the control logic is able to write/read values into/from the registers of one arithmetical module, while the others keep on running. The advantage of

---
[1] The size of one BRAM is actually 18 Kbit, but it is difficult to exploit the upper most bits for other tasks besides parity bits.

Chapter 6. Novel flexible and efficient co-processor architecture for server applications

this approach is its high simplicity. However, it requires additional hardware in form of the input and output registers containing only redundant data. Furthermore, additional cycles are needed for copying this data, during which the concerned module is stalled.

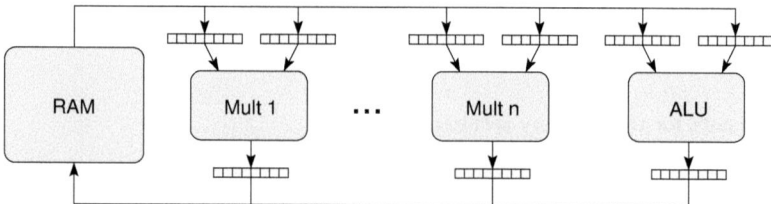

Figure 6.5.: Conventional memory architecture

As example for the overhead, consider modules supporting a maximum width of 3072 bit, which is the maximum supported in this work. For the two input and the output registers, a total of 9216 flipflops – i.e., 4608 slices – would be needed, which is about 34% of the flipflops available on the FPGA used for the prototype[2]. Assuming a word-width of 32 bit, copying the input values to the registers takes at least 192 cycles and 96 cycles for copying the results back to memory.

Utilized parallel memory architecture

This work rather employs the memory architecture from [58, 60], which allows to fetch the values directly from memory when needed. For this, each modular multiplier module is assigned its own storage, which is connected via the first memory port of the BRAMs. Therefore, the multiplier modules do not have to share their memory accesses with each other and registers to store values from memory in are not required. The module for the modular arithmetic besides the multiplication utilizes the second port of each BRAM to access the data independently from the multiplier modules. Note that this would not be possible using distributed memory, as it does not offer two truly independent memory ports.

Resulting from the direct memory connection the resource usage is kept low and no cycles are needed for copying. Instead the architecture exploits BRAMs, which are utilized anyway to store the input values and the final results. Furthermore, because the multiplier modules do not compete for memory access, the execution time may scale with the number of multipliers. Thus, by adding additional modular multiplier modules, the execution time is reduced as long as this is not prohibited by data dependencies of the algorithms.

However, because of the direct memory connection each multiplier module can only access its own memory block. Intermediate results needed by one multiplier, but gen-

---

[2]It is also possible to use BRAMs as registers, in which case the percentage of the resource usage is not as high. However, the data in these registers can not be accessed as flexibly and is still redundantly stored.

erated by another one, have to be copied between memory blocks by the module for the remaining modular arithmetic. Therefore, copying is needed to keep the different memory blocks consistent. However, because the storage for temporary values does not always have to be consistent, the amount of copying can by kept reasonably low. For example, no copying is needed, if the result of a multiplication is used on the same multiplier it was generated on. Furthermore, the scalability is not affected by this copying, because all memory blocks may be accessed in parallel by the modular arithmetic performing the copying. Additionally, in the prototype implementation the algorithms for point addition and doubling and most algorithms for the operations in the extension field could be scheduled in a way that avoids copying except for that during modular additions and subtractions, which already contain copying anyway. In these modular operations, both the not-reduced and the reduced results are computed and stored into different memory blocks in parallel and copying is required to write the correct result over the incorrect one, see Algorithm 3.1 and Algorithm 3.2, respectively.

The direct memory connection results in an increase of the amount of required BRAMs, as each parallel multiplier features its own memory. This is, however, preferable to the large amount of registers the conventional approach would need. Furthermore, the algorithms on the next higher level become slightly more complicated as they have to employ the modular operations in parallel and must keep the memory blocks roughly consistent. But this increase is not very high, as the control logic for the conventional architecture has to copy data into the proper registers and employs the operations in parallel, too. Besides, this increase in complexity concerns mainly software, where the effects are only minor. Note that the additional work load does usually not affect runtime, because it may be executed in parallel to the multiplications.

Figure 6.6 shows the ModArith core, also highlighting the memory architecture including its connections to the controlling *scheme controller*. The scheme controller may read and write data into/from the two *memories*. Furthermore, it can issue commands to and read out the status from the module for the *remaining modular arithmetic*, which is explained in more detail in Section 6.2.3. Thus, the modular arithmetic provides an unified interface for the processor, which, therefore, does not have to access the modular multipliers *ModMult* directly. Instead, the commands to the multipliers are received by the remaining modular arithmetic, which sends them on. The same is true in the opposite direction for the status signals from the multipliers. Thus, for example, the scheme controller may start parallel multiplications on both multipliers, then execute two modular additions in sequence using the modular arithmetic, wait for the multiplications to finish, and continue with further operations.

Both modular multipliers are directly connected to one *Memory*, allowing it to read data from it anytime. The second port of the memory is shared via the multiplexer MUX by the modular arithmetic and the scheme controller. This is possible, because the scheme controller does not need to – and in fact should not – access the memory during the runtime of the modular arithmetic. This is reflected by using the *Busy*-signal of the modular arithmetic to control the multiplexer.

Note that it would be possible to utilize time division multiplex access to provide the memory with a third or even a fourth port as described in [106], thus, allowing concurrent

Chapter 6. Novel flexible and efficient co-processor architecture for server applications

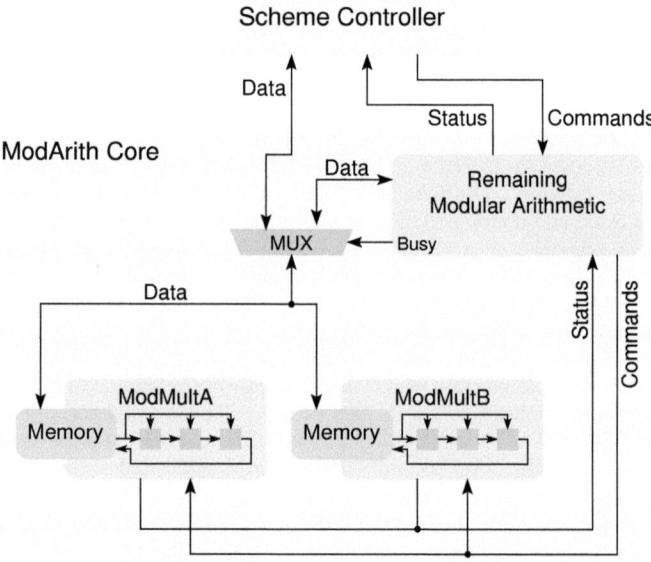

Figure 6.6.: ModArith core highlighting the memory architecture

access from both the processor and the modular arithmetic. But, by disconnecting the processor from the memory while the modular arithmetic is working the robustness is increased.

6.2.3. Remaining modular arithmetic

The module for the remaining modular arithmetic provides the unified interface of the modular arithmetic core to the outside world, i.e., the scheme controllers, see Section 6.4. For this, it controls the parallel multiplier instances and, furthermore, realizes some basic modular functions. The modular operations not contained in the modular arithmetic module are implemented in software utilizing modular operations.

Copying

The copy operation is one of the most basic functionalities of the module for the remaining modular arithmetic. It copies data from a memory block to the same or another memory block. In particular, this is necessary to copy intermediate results between the memories of different multipliers, because each multiplier is only able to access its own memory.

6.2. Modular arithmetic core

Comparison

The comparison operation executes an "is equal"-comparison of two different sections of data in memory. The scheme controller may read the result, i.e., whether the contents of both are the same or not, from the appropriate status bit.

Modular multiplication

The interface provided by the modular arithmetic module for the multiplication consists of one separate opcode for each multiplier instance and one status bit indicating whether the multiplier is currently busy or not. To allow fast restart of consecutive multiplications on the same multiplier, it is possible to issue a multiply-command before the corresponding multiplier is finished. Then the modular arithmetic module "goes to sleep" and waits exclusively for this multiplier to end its execution and, then, directly starts the new multiplication. Note that in this state the module for the remaining modular arithmetic module is not accessible. This behavior also prevents problems which could otherwise arise from the start of a multiplication before the last one is finished.

Modular addition and subtraction

The modular addition and subtraction is realized roughly according to Algorithm 3.1 and Algorithm 3.1 from Section 3.2, respectively. Contrary to above algorithms, the not-reduced result $c = a \pm b$ and the reduced result $c = a \pm b \mp q$ are computed in parallel at the same time and stored in the memories of different multipliers. The *if*-instruction is then substituted by copying the correct result over the incorrect one.

Modular division by 2

The realization of the modular division by 2 is according to Algorithm 3.3 from Section 3.2. The result is directly written to the designated memory location.

Modular inversion

The modular inversion is not implemented in the ModArith core, but on the scheme controller using modular multiplications. It is only included here, because it is a modular operation and it is important, how those are realized. The modular inversion is substituted by a modular exponentiation, see Section 3.2, which is rather control flow intensive, as it does not operate on the words of the integer values directly, but rather utilizes modular multiplications.

Modular square root

Similar to the modular inversion, the modular square root is calculated by a modular exponentiation, see Section 3.2. Therefore, it is implemented on the scheme controller, too, using the same approach.

6.3. Auxiliary function core

For the complete execution of public key schemes, some cryptographic auxiliary functions are required. In Section 6.1.2, it was decided to realize these functions, namely, symmetric en-/decryption, a hash function, and a random number generator together as a compact core. To gain this compactness the block cipher AES, see [83], is used as basis for all three functions. By sharing a module for AES between the auxiliary functions, they may be realized with a smaller resource usage than by implementing them independently. By choosing an area-optimized AES-design from literature the compactness of the auxiliary function core is further aided.

6.4. Scheme controllers

In the proposed co-processor architecture, all operations above the abstraction level of the modular arithmetic, which are needed during a cryptographic scheme, are realized in software, see Section 6.1. For this task, general purpose processors are utilized controlling the ModArith cores. Thus, these processors realize the three middle abstraction levels intermediate algebraic structures, cryptographic main operation, and cryptographic scheme in software.

As shown in Figure 6.2 each ModArith core is assigned to one general purpose processor. Generally, however, it would be possible to utilize one processor to control two ore more of these cores, thus, saving hardware resource. Given enough computational power of the processor, this could be possible without a big increase in execution time, because the processor waits most of the time anyway.

But then, the software needs to be able to support the concurrency of the hardware. The usual solution for such problems, namely, exploiting multiple software threads, proves prohibitive expensive, because a thread switch requires too many cycles. For example, a thread switch on the PowerPC on the FPGA used for the prototype implementation with the supplied *xil_kernel* library needs more than 1000 cycles. This is too long, because most modular operations are shorter. Thus, a customized program would be needed, which somehow keeps track of multiple parallel command sequences. This, in turn, would complicate the realization of the schemes in software and waste one of its main advantages, namely, the ease of implementation and maintenance. Furthermore, this approach does not allow truly simultaneous starts of modular operations, because the communication via the bus takes at least a few cycles.

6.5. Central core

To handle communication with the outside world and to control all other modules, a further general purpose processor is used as central core. Although these tasks could in theory be distributed over the scheme controller, it is beneficial to exploit one dedicated instance instead. Firstly, this way the outside world has one fixed communication partner and it helps hiding implementation details. Secondly, the additional tasks for the scheme controllers would hinder the execution of the cryptographic schemes and lead to a certain overhead. Thirdly, this clear division of the functionality eases implementation and maintenance.

Chapter 7.
Prototype implementation

This chapter describes the prototype implementation used to evaluate the feasibility of the proposed co-processor architecture. It was realized on an XUP2P board as described in Chapter 5. For design and synthesis the Xilinx EDK and ISE software tools were used, both in version 9.1. Single building blocks and a prior variant of the implementation were already published in [58, 59, 61, 95, 79].

This chapter starts by presenting the supported functionality of the prototype and by providing an overview on its architecture. Then, the inner workings of the different cores types are explained in more detail. Finally, the execution flow of an RSA encryption is described as an example.

7.1. Supported functionality

The prototype implementation is restricted to common public key cryptography schemes for RSA and ECC with security levels between 80 and 128 bit, see below. In this context a security level of 80 bit means that the probability to find the correct key by guessing is $1/2^{80}$. Table 7.1 shows the RSA and ECC schemes supported in this work. As example for the flexibility of the architecture and its upgradeability, a PBC scheme, namely the BLS scheme, was also implemented. However, because the PBC scheme was intended as proof-of-concept only, the prototype supports PBC just with a security level of 80 bit.

Table 7.1.: Public key schemes realized in the prototype

Function	RSA	ECC	PBC
Encryption/Decryption	RSAES-OAEP[100]	ECIES[42]	–
Signing/Verification	RSASSA-PSS[100]	ECDSA[43]	BLS[16]

Today, the recommended security level ranges from 80 bit for medium term to 128 bit for long term security, see [116, 37][1]. This range of security levels was chosen for the prototype implementation of the co-processor. An increase of the range is possible with relatively small changes, mainly, in the ModArith cores, in the software parts, and

---
[1]Note that [63] offers more precise numbers, however, those may not be mapped as easily to the usual standard recommendations.

in the size of the memory². Table 7.2 shows the respective key-lengths required by the different cryptographic approaches to guarantee the desired security level.

Table 7.2.: Different security bit-lengths and the resulting key-length

Security (bit)	Symmetric cryptography	Hash	Public key cryptography		
			RSA	ECC	PBC
80	80	160	1024	160	160 and 512
96	96	192	1536	192	–
112	112	224	2048	224	–
128	128	256	3072	256	–

As can be seen from Table 7.2, the required bit-widths for the modular operations are between 160 bits and 3072 bits. Thus, the hardware core for the modular arithmetic needs to be able to support computations on integers in this range. Note that the bit-lengths for PBC is 160 for n and 512 for q, respectively, as explained in Section 4.1.3.

For a complete scheme execution, some auxiliary functions are needed besides the modular calculations, namely, symmetric encryption, hash function, and random number generation. Table 7.3 shows which auxiliary functions are required in the supported schemes.

Table 7.3.: Auxiliary functions needed for different public key schemes

Scheme	Symmetric encryption	Hash function	Random number generation
RSAES-OAEP	–	✓	✓
RSASSA-PSS	–	✓	✓
ECDSA	–	✓	✓
ECIES	✓	✓	✓
BLS	–	✓	✓

Parameters sets for ECC and PBC

In contrast to RSA, the mathematical background of ECC and PBC is more complex and these two approaches require parameters defining valid elliptic curve. These parameters are different to the parameters of RSA, as they are independent from the key generation and may even be shared by several users. Because the generation of these parameter sets describing elliptic curves is not a central topic of this work, such sets from literature were used.

---

[2]Note that the prototype implementation is already able to compute ECC over the NIST curves P-384 and P-521, i.e., over numbers with bit-widths of 384 and 521, respectively. This was, however, not examined further, because the equivalent bit-widths for RSA are beyond the maximum bit-width of the prototype implementation.

For ECC the most common coordinate system is the Jacobian projective coordinate system, which is standardized in IEEE P1363, see [42]. This standard also contains the necessary algorithms for ECC. In particular, the algorithm for point addition is taken from [42], see Algorithm 3.7. The algorithm for point doubling shown in Algorithm 3.8, however, is taken form [39]. This is because special curves with the Weierstraß-coefficient $a = -3$ were used in the prototype allowing a faster doubling.

This fits well, as the parameter sets defining the elliptic curves were taken from [85], where this optimization is suggested, too. Unfortunately, for curves with a bit-lengths of 160 bit, [85] does not provide parameters sets. Therefore, the LiDIA-library, see [44], was used to generate a suitable parameter set.

In contrast to ECC, PBC is still in its research phase, thus, there is not yet a standardized form. The parameter set utilized to execute the BLS scheme is taken from the PBC Library, see [68], where this type of curve is denoted *Type A curves*. This and the corresponding mathematical background are described in the PhD thesis [69] from the same author. The concrete parameter values may be found in Appendix A. Note that the code of the PBC Library was extremely helpful for understanding many aspects concerning the implementation of PBC, although it was not possible to reuse it in its original form, because of the different realization platforms.

7.2. Co-processor architecture

Figure 7.1 provides an elaborate view on the concrete architecture of the prototype implementation of the proposed co-processor. In contrast to Figure 6.2, it also contains realization details, e.g., the different core types for the general purpose processors or how the instruction and data storage is arranged. Note that Figure 7.1 shows a design variant with four parallel scheme controllers, because this was the maximum number fitting onto the available resources. As explained below, variants with two and three parallel scheme controllers were also tested. It would also be possible to instantiate five or more parallel scheme controllers on a larger FPGA type featuring more reconfigurable logic and, in particular, more on-chip memory.

For each parallel scheme execution, the co-processor comprises one *modular arithmetic core* (ModArith), which is responsible for the operations on the lowest abstraction level. The scheme controller assigned to each ModArith core is realized by a *MicroBlaze* processor (MB), which is the soft-core type available on the Virtex-II Pro platform, see Chapter 5. For the connection between a MicroBlaze processor and its ModArith core the Fast Simplex Link (*FSL*) is exploited. Note that the MicroBlaze processor was utilized to implement the scheme controllers, because it may be instantiated multiple times. This way, different configurations with different numbers of parallel scheme executions may be examined. In contrast, the exploitation of the PowerPC cores would allow a maximum of only two schemes in parallel.

The *instruction* and *data memories* for the MicroBlaze processors (*IM* and *DM*, respectively) are connected via the Local Memory Bus (*LMB*). They consist of BRAMs, whose dual-ported nature allows to share a single instruction memory between two soft-

Chapter 7. Prototype implementation

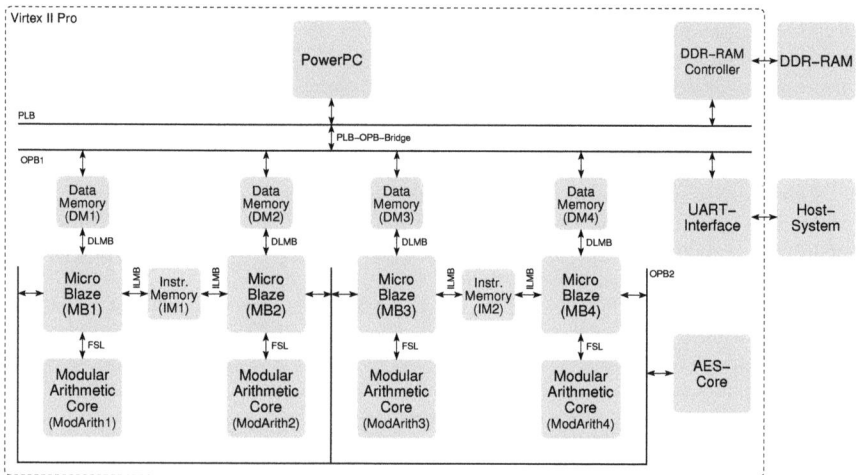

Figure 7.1.: Detailed view on the new co-processor architecture

cores. This reduces the amount of memory blocks necessary for a single scheme controller. A similar sharing is not possible for the data memory because of two reasons: Firstly, to allow independent scheme execution in all soft-cores, each needs its own independent data memory. Secondly, because the data memory operates as shared memory between the scheme controllers and the central core, the second memory port is utilized to allow access by the central core, namely the PowerPC. The size of a single instruction memory is 64 KByte, while one data memory contains only 16 KByte. Note that for design variants with an odd amount of parallel scheme controllers, a full instruction memory is still needed for the last controller, although only one port is exploited while the other one stays unused.

For the auxiliary functions needed during the scheme execution, the MicroBlaze cores utilize the *AES core*. It may be accessed via the second Open Processor Bus (*OPB2*).

The central core of the co-processor is realized using one of the two available *PowerPC* cores. Although an additional MicroBlaze processor should be fast enough to take over the control tasks, the exploitation of a PowerPC core saves slices. The instruction and data memory of the central core resides in the off-chip *DDR-RAM*, which may be accessed via the *DDR-RAM Controller* connected to the Processor Local Bus *(PLB)*. For the communication with the *Host-System*, the PowerPC utilizes the *UART-Interface*, which may be accessed using the first Open Processor Bus (*OPB1*) via the *PLB-OPB-Bridge*. The communication with the soft-cores is possible by accessing their data memories. This allows to provide them with new parameters and to send them commands.

Note that some design decisions make sense for a proof-of-concept realization only. Firstly, no off-chip memory should be used, as this opens additional avenues of attack.

This, however, would require additional on-chip memory or the removal of some functionality. A previous version of the co-processor presented in [79], which only offers RSA and ECC schemes does fit completely into the available on-chip memory of the exploited Virtex-II Pro FPGA. The inclusion of PBC for the variant described in this work required more memory and made the use of the off-chip memory necessary. It would also be possible to utilize a larger FPGA offering more on-chip memory. Secondly, the communication with the host system should rather be implemented with a faster interface, e.g., an Ethernet connection. This was, however, not done, as this connection did not constitute a bottleneck.

7.3. Modular arithmetic core

The realization of the ModArith core follows the proposed design very tightly, see Figure 6.6. Therefore, this depiction should be used to gain an overview on the realization of the core. The main difference is that the communication between scheme controller and ModArith is realized with an FSL.

Using this FSL connection to its ModArith core, the associated MicroBlaze processor may read from and write to the internal memory of the ModArith core. Furthermore, the FSL may be utilized to issue commands the ModArith core, thus, starting modular operations working on the values stored in the internal memory. Finally, the status, i.e., whether an operation is still running and the result of a comparison, may be read using the FSL.

The communication interface between MicroBlaze processor and the ModArith core is explained below in detail. This is followed by an overview on the memory configuration, which is slightly different for RSA and ECC and must handle the two memory banks belonging to the two multiplier instances. Then, the realization of the modular operations is explored, starting with the modular multiplication featuring short pipelines and concluded by the remaining modular operations.

7.3.1. Interface of the ModArith core

The connection via the FSL allows 32 bit words to be written to and read from the ModArith core. Thus, the interface of the ModArith core has to enable the processor to read and write from/into the memory, to send commands, and to check the state using just 32 bit words.

All access types to the ModArith core consist of two words transferred over the FSL. The first word is always written by the MicroBlaze processor and initiates the access. The second word is either written or read, depending on the type of the access. Figure 7.2(a) shows the structure of the first word send to the ModArith core. The bits *write*, *read*, or *status*, of which at most one may be set, result in the execution of the associated operation. In that case, the content of the opcode is ignored. If none of these three bits is set, the access is interpreted as command for a modular operation. Then a second word is expected, which is depicted in Figure 7.2(b).

Chapter 7. Prototype implementation

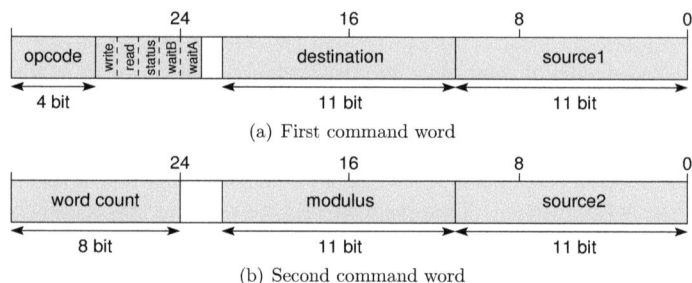

Figure 7.2.: Structure of the command words for the ModArith-core

In the following the behavior of the possible access types is explained in more detail.

Read Access For this access type, the bit *read* has to be set. The address from which the data is to be read is expected in bits 0 to 9 of the field *source1*. The bits *waitA* and *waitB* may be set, but are ignored. The actual data word is returned in the next read operation of the FSL. Note that bit 10 of the field *source1* is ignored, because only memory bank A may be read as described in Section 7.3.2.

Write Access For this access type, the bit *write* has to be set. The address to which the data is to be written is expected in bits 0 to 9 of the field *source1*. The bits *waitA* and *waitB* may be set, but are ignored. The actual data word to be written must be send as the next write operation of the FSL. Again, bit 10 of the field *source1* is ignored, because the data is written into both memory banks, see Section 7.3.2.

GetStatus For this access type, the bit *status* has to be set. The actual status word is returned in the next read operation of the FSL. In case the bits *waitA* and/or *waitB* are set, the following read operation of the FSL delays the execution of the MicroBlaze code until the multiplier instance *ModMultA* and/or *ModMultB*, respectively, finishes execution.

The structure of the status word returned by the ModArith core is depicted in Figure 7.3. Bit 0 signifies, whether the modular arithmetic besides the multipliers is currently running, see Section 7.3.4. Because the FSL should delay execution of the MicroBlaze code until these operations are finished, it should never occur that this bit is set. Bit 8 and bit 16 indicate, whether the modular multipliers ModMultA and/or ModMultB, respectively, are currently running. Although waiting for the completion of a multiplication may be realized this way using busy waiting, it is more elegant to set the bit *waitA* and/or *waitB* and leave the actual waiting to the FSL as described above. Bit 24, finally, contains the result of the last comparison operation. It is set, if the numbers compared were equal and not set otherwise.

Command For this access type, the three bits *write*, *read*, and *status* must not be set. The bits *waitA* and *waitB* may be set, but are ignored. Because the necessary pa-

7.3. Modular arithmetic core

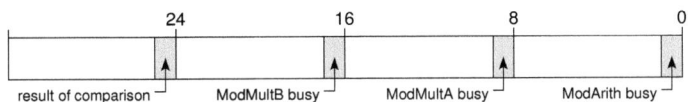

Figure 7.3.: Structure of the status word of the ModArith core

rameters for a command do not fit into a single word, a subsequent write operation to the FSL is necessary providing the ModArith core with the second command word, see Figure 7.2(b). The fields *destination*, *source1*, *source2*, and *modulus* have to be filled with the 11 bit addresses of the respective value in the memory of the ModArith core. Not all of these fields are needed for all commands, which is detailed in Table 7.4.

After the second command word is read, the opcode is forwarded to the finite state machine actually executing the modular operations. Furthermore – except for multiplications – the acknowledgment of the write operation to the FSL is delayed until the issued modular operation is finished. This delay has the advantage that the FSL is doing the actual waiting and it has not to be implemented as busy waiting in the MicroBlaze code. The immediate acknowledgment of the write operation in case of a multiplication enables a continuation of the MicroBlaze code and allows to execute operations in parallel to a multiplication.

Figure 7.4 depicts the finite state machine controlling the FSL connection. The start state is *ReadOne*. Note that "FSL does not accept word" means that the associated queue is full and the ModArith core has to wait until the MicroBlaze processor reads something from the FSL. This case is only included for robustness, as it does not occur in practice, but the soft-core is rather waiting for the ModArith core to transfer control back.

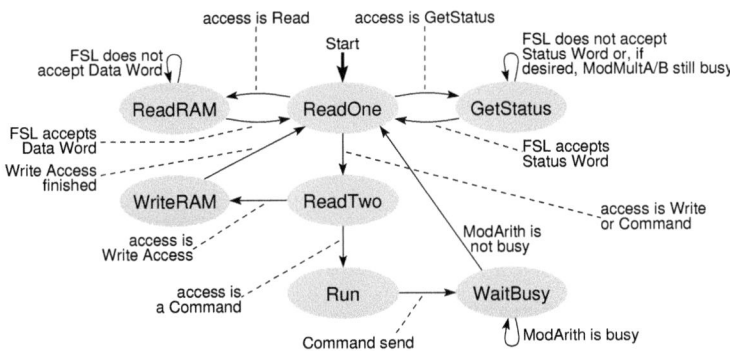

Figure 7.4.: FSM for the FSL connection of the ModArith core

The different operations the ModArith core is able to execute are depicted in Table 7.4. The first column contains the bit string to be used as opcode in the first command word, see Figure 7.2(a). The operation associated with each bit string is provided in the second column. An "✓" in columns three to six illustrates that the address of the destination, of first and second source, and of the modulus, respectively, is expected as parameter. If "–" is given, the value of the respective parameter is ignored. The last column, finally, describes the command, in particular, whether it changes the data at the destination address of only one or both memory banks. The internal workings of the different operations are explained in more detail in Section 7.3.3 for the multiplication and in Section 7.3.4 for the remaining modular operations.

Table 7.4.: Commands supported by the ModArith core

Op-code	Command	Is parameter needed?				Function
		dest	src1	src2	mod	
0000	ModNop	–	–	–	–	no operation
0001	reserved	–	–	–	–	–
0010	ModCopy	✓	✓	–	–	copies data from *src1* to *dest* changes only one memory bank
0011	ModCmp	–	✓	✓	–	compares data of *src1* and *src2* result may be read using GetStatus
0100	ModAdd	✓	✓	✓	✓	modular addition changes both memory banks
0100	ModSub	✓	✓	✓	✓	modular subtraction changes both memory banks
0110	reserved	–	–	–	–	–
0111	ModDiv2	✓	✓	–	✓	modular division by 2 changes only one memory bank
1000–1011	reserved	–	–	–	–	–
1100	ModMultA	✓	✓	✓	✓	modular multiplication on multiplier A changes only one memory bank
1100	ModMultB	✓	✓	✓	✓	modular multiplication on multiplier B changes only one memory bank
1110–1111	reserved	–	–	–	–	–

7.3.2. Memory configuration

As described in Section 6.2.2, the ModArith core comprises its own storage for the values its operations work on. This storage is the memory directly assigned to the modular multipliers. Because the prototype implementation utilizes two parallel modular multipliers, the storage in the ModArith core consists of two memory banks as illustrated in Figure 7.5(a).

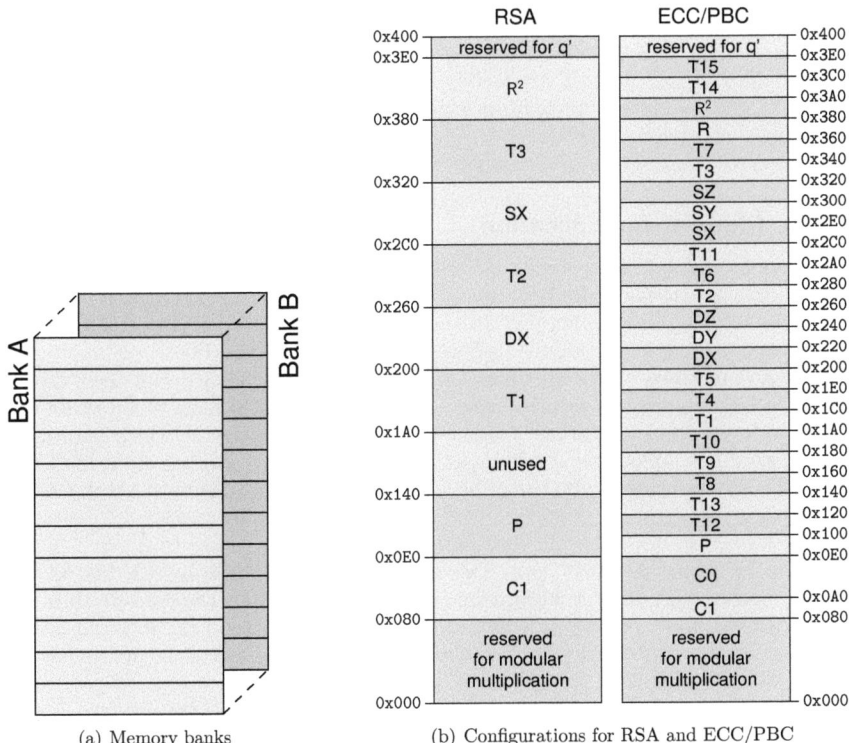

Figure 7.5.: Visualization of ModArith memory

As both memory banks should essentially contain the same data, only the first bank is visible to the outside, i.e., the MicroBlaze processor. Thus, with a write access from the soft-core the corresponding address in both banks is written. A read access, however, returns only the content of this address in bank A. Internally, most modular operations are able to access both memory banks. Therefore, it is possible to transfer data between both banks for the modular multiplications, which are the only operations not able to access both banks. In this context, it is also important that the modular addition and subtraction write their result to the output memory location in both banks, while all other operations change only one bank, see Section 7.3.1. For the creation of feasible schedules, this has to be kept in mind, see Section 7.5.5.

Chapter 7. Prototype implementation

For a feasible memory configuration, it is important that it enables all supported schemes. Thus, Figure 7.5(b) shows the configurations for RSA and ECC/PBC. Each memory location for RSA has a size of 3072 bit, while each location for ECC contains only 1024 bit. Thus, 3 ECC memory locations fit into a single RSA memory location. The naming scheme allows to use the same addresses for both cases with additional addresses for the smaller memory areas of ECC/PBC.

The addresses *DX* and *SX* are mainly used as destination and source, respectively. For ECC, these addresses are split into three smaller locations used to store the three coordinates of a point. The addresses *T?* are used for temporary values. Note that the temporary values *T11* to *T15* are only needed for the PBC scheme.

7.3.3. Modular multiplication

The modular multiplication is the most critical operation of the ModArith core. Because of the limitations to parallelization, it is to be implemented using the pipelined approach according to [114], see Section 6.2. In contrast to [114], however, it should work in a word-based manner exploiting the dedicated multipliers on the FPGA.

Such a word-based pipelined realization may be found in [52, 51]. But these designs require a more customized memory access as available in the memory architecture used in the prototype implementation. Thus, a different design was needed, which features the desired word-based pipelining while complying to the memory interface of the ModArith core. The resulting realization may be found in [95] and is described shortly in the following.

As described in Section 6.2.2, the multiplier has exclusive access to the first port of the memory in the ModArith core. This means that all values to be read and written by the pipeline have to be transferred over this memory port. The data-width of this port is set to 16 bit, because it is half of the word-width of the FSL. It would also be possible to use a word-width of 17 bit, but then the word-borders of the multipliers and the FSL would differ.

The connections between the memory and the pipeline stages are depicted in Figure 7.6. These connections are controlled by an FSM, which also fetches the values from memory at the appropriate time. The register *Reg* in front of the first stage reduces the longest path and, thus, decreases the minimum cycle period. Values from the register may be fed directly into the first stage or via additional inputs directly into latter stages.

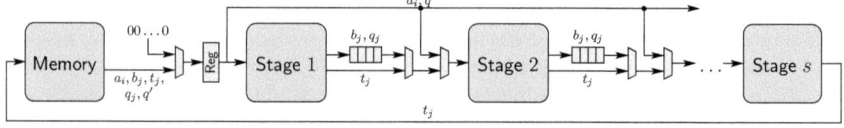

Figure 7.6.: Pipeline architecture of the modular multiplication

Each stage has to compute n steps of the inner loop to compute its i-th step of the outer loop. Each step j takes five clock cycles, because five memory accesses are needed to compute the intermediate result $t_j(i) := a_i \cdot b_j + u_i \cdot q_j + t_{j+1}(i-1) + carry$. The value $t_j(i)$ denotes the j-th word of t in step i of the outer loop. Remember that n and s are the number of words to be computed and the number of instantiated stages, respectively. j denotes the counter required for the inner loop to calculate line 4 of Algorithm 3.5 in a word-by-word manner.

The stages after the first one could compute their results in less cycles, because they get their input values from previous stages and not from memory. This, however, would lead to problems with storing the results of the last stage in memory, which must be coordinated with the read accesses. Because this has to work for all stage and word counts, it was decided that a stage needs five cycles for the calculation of each step j.

The shift registers buffer b_j and q_j for ten cycles until the next stage needs them, while t_j may be directly passed on to the next stage. The ten cycles delay are required, because the next stage needs b_j and q_j together with the intermediate result $t_{j+1}(i-1)$, which is calculated by the previous stage two steps of the inner loop later. As each step of the inner loop takes five cycles, see below, the delay is ten cycles.

During the five cycles each stage executes the memory accesses listed below. Because the structure of the stages is the same except for the last one, they do not know whether the input values come from memory or from a previous stage. Note that the read operation from memory actually has to be executed one cycle earlier to feed the values into the register Reg, from where it is actually read by the stages.

1. In the first cycle the stage reads a_i, if it needs it. Remember that the finite state machine connecting the stages fetches the required a_i from memory in time.

2. In the second cycle each stage reads the word b_j. It is used in the multiplication $a_i \cdot b_j$ and passed on via the shift registers to the next stage.

3. In the third cycle each stage reads the intermediate result $t_{j+1}(i-1)$. This value is added to the intermediate result the stage is calculating, which is then passed on to the next stage.

4. In the fourth cycle the intermediate result $t_j(i)$ of the last stage is written into memory.

5. In the fifth cycle each stage reads q_j. This is needed for the multiplication $u_i \cdot q_j$ and also passed on via the shift registers to next stage.

Note that the designated memory access is not executed in all cycles, but that this rather represents the time slot, in which it may be done. For example each stage does read a_i only once at the beginning of its i-th step. If all stages have read their a_i and are not yet finished with their i-th step, nothing is read in the first cycle. Further note that u_i is computed together with the first result $t_0(i)$ in the first 5 cycles of each stage.

The interior of each stages exhibits the data paths depicted in Figure 7.7 and is controlled by its own finite state machine. Note that if the path-widths in Figure 7.7 do not fit, the values are filled from the left with 0.

Chapter 7. Prototype implementation

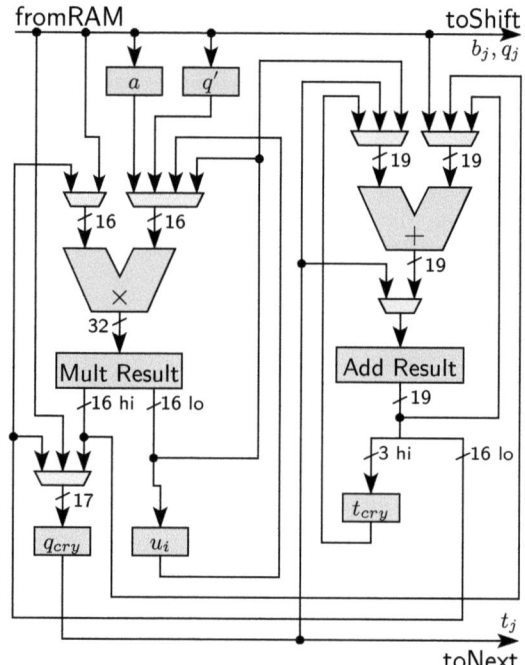

Figure 7.7.: Data path of a single pipeline stage

The overall execution time of one modular multiplication is $5n \cdot \lceil \frac{n}{s} \rceil + 10 \lceil \frac{n}{s} \rceil + 10s - 5$ clock cycles, Additionally, 3 to $5n - 2$ clock cycles are required to calculate the correction in lines 6 to 8 of Algorithm 3.5, depending on how fast the comparison reaches a conclusive result.

7.3.4. Remaining modular operations

As described in Section 6.2.3, all operations of the ModArith core – except for the multiplication – are executed by the same finite state machine using the mathematical algorithms introduced in Section 3.2. To provide an unified interface for all operations, this finite state machine is responsible for controlling the modular multiplications as well.

The internals of the operations are presented in the following. The lengths of the memory areas operated on must be given as word-count in the second command word, see Figure 7.2(b), where one word has a width of 32 bit.

ModNop

This command executes no operation and changes no internal value. The state machine stays in the *waiting* state and may be given another command in the next cycle.

ModCopy

This command copies the data in the memory following the address *source1* to the memory following the address *destination*. The copying is executed word-by-word and only that memory bank is changed, in which *destination* is located.

ModCmp

This command compares the contents of the memory locations following the addresses *source1* and *source2*. If the contents of both memory locations are equal, the output port `cmp_result` of the state machine is set to '1', otherwise it is set to '0'. The value of this port may be read out as part of the status word.

ModAdd/ModSub

The command `ModAdd` executes a modular addition of the contents of the memory locations *source1* and *source2*. The data at the location *modulus* is used as modulus for this operation. The result is written into the memory at the address *destination* in both memory banks.

Internally, both the not-reduced and the reduced result are computed at the same time. Former result is written into the memory location *destination* in memory bank A, while latter result is written to the same address in bank B. After checking which result is correct, this result is copied over the incorrect one. Note that this copying reuses the parts of the state machine intended for `ModCopy`.

The command `ModSub` executes a modular subtraction of *source2* from *source1* using a similar approach.

ModDiv2

This operation computes a modular division by 2 of the value at the memory location *source1* using the address *modulus* as modulus. For this, the state machine checks, whether the value to be divided is odd or even. Then, either the value at the address of the input *source1* or the sum of this value and that at the address *modulus* is shifted one bit to the right and, subsequently, written to the memory location *destination* as result, see Algorithm 3.3.

ModMultA/ModMultB

Essentially, these commands start the respective multiplier, if possible. For this, they check the state of the multiplier. If the multiplier is busy, the state machine waits for it to become idle. Then – or if it was already idle – the multiplication is started and

Chapter 7. Prototype implementation

the state machine returns into the waiting state, thus, allowing the execution of other operations, while the multiplier is working. This approach allows the controlling instance to issue a multiplication while another one is still running, which leads to a minimum idle time for the multiplier.

7.4. Auxiliary function core

For the prototype implementation in this work, the core from [61] is used to execute the auxiliary cryptographic functions presented in Section 4.4. It provides this functionality with a low resource usage as the following overview on other compact realizations shows. Subsequently, the architecture of the AES core from [61] is presented.

The minimum bit-widths for the provided functions follow from Table 7.2. Thus, the key-length for the symmetric en-/decryption must be at least 128 bit. Larger key-lengths were also implemented, because the key-length for the block cipher must be 256 bit to allow the necessary length of the hash function. The length of an output block of the hash function has to be at least 256 bit. For the output block-length of the cryptographically secure random number generator (CSRNG), finally, there are no critical constraints, therefore, it was set to 256 bit.

7.4.1. Overview on other realizations

Table 7.5 provides the resource usage figures of compact realizations for the auxiliary functions from literature. Note that some tolerance is needed for the comparison of the slice counts, because the designs were implemented on different Xilinx FPGA types. This also concerns the size of the BRAMs, which is just 4 Kbit where marked with "*" and 18 Kbit otherwise.

Table 7.5.: Resource usage of different AES implementations

Ref	Application	#slices	#BRAM	FPGA type
[3]	AES with CCM	487	4	Spartan-3
[40]	MD5/SHA-1/224/256	526	1	Virtex-II Pro
[115]	RNG	307	1*	Virtex-E
[94]	AES (CTR-mode), Hash	823	n/a	Virtex-II
[19]	AES module	222	3*	Spartan-II
[99]	AES module	146	3	Virtex-II
[35]	AES module	124	2*	Spartan-II

The design from [3] provides AES encryption with CCM-mode (Counter-Mode with CBC-MAC). Note that the Cipher Block Chaining-mode (CBC) for the Message Authentication Code (MAC) is not used in this work, thus, the AES encryption from [3] contains functionality not present in this work. An industrial solution for a hash function with an output bit-width of 256 (here SHA-256) geared for compactness is proposed in [40]. A random number generator (RNG), finally, is presented in [115].

The resource costs of these three cores amount to 1320 slices and 6 BRAMs, if possible synergies or additional overhead for buses are ignored. In contrast, the architecture from [61], which is used in this work, centers on an AES module shared between the auxiliary functions. Utilizing this approach, it is able to provide similar functionality using only 916 slices and 5 BRAMs.

Another example for the approach of sharing an AES module between different functions may be found in [94], which offers AES encryption with counter-mode and a hash function, see [66] and [23], respectively. The AES core utilized in this work extends this approach by also including a CSRNG, see Section 4.4.4, and employing an AES module optimized for area as central element. Three possible AES modules are described in [19, 99, 35]. For the core from [61] the module from [19] was chosen. The solution from [99] was disregarded, as it requires more memory, which is needed as instruction and data memory in the prototype implementation. In turn, the realization from [35] was refused, because it exhibits an about 75 times smaller throughput.

7.4.2. Architecture overview and interface

The 32 bit data path of the AES core is shown in Figure 7.8. The central element is the *AES module* consisting of the *key scheduler* and the *encrypt*-unit. The dual-ported *interface memory* is used to store most of the internal values and to exchange data with the host system. Via its first port data may be fed into and read from the *auxiliary units*, while the second port is attached to the *bus* and to the key scheduler, which has only read access to the memory. The management of the data exchange between the host system and the AES core is supervised by the *controller*, which also controls the operations of the different hardware units.

The host system issues a command by first writing the necessary parameters into the memory and then sending a command word to the controller. The configuration of the memory visible from the host system is depicted in Table 7.6.

The first column displays at which address the different memory locations start, while their length in words is given in the second column. The third column contains the names used later on to refer to the respective memory locations. Columns four to six, finally, indicate for which of the three functions the memory location is used.

The interface of the AES core provides the following four commands:

En-/Decrypt This command en-/decrypts the content of the memory location *data*. The key, which may have a length of either 128 bit, 192 bit, or 256 bit, is expected in the memory location *key*. The *nonce* allows to initialize the counter used in the counter-mode encryption with an arbitrary value. Note that the host system may only set the three most significant words, while the least significant word is always initialized with 1 by the AES core.

If the amount of data is too big to completely fit into the available memory, the AES core is able to perform the operation in multiple passes inspecting one fragment

Chapter 7. Prototype implementation

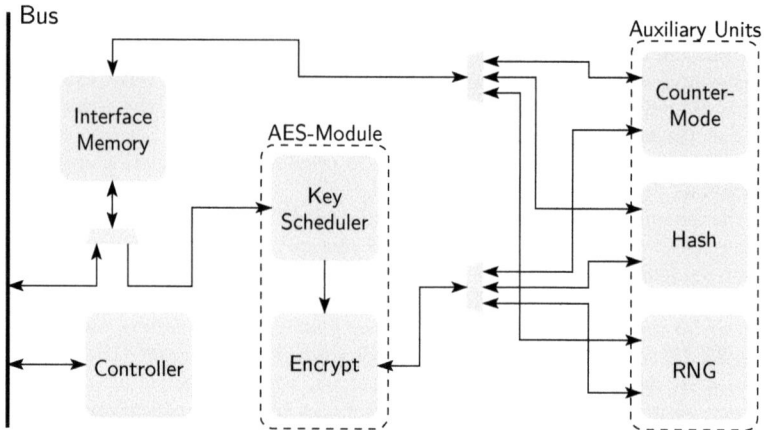

Figure 7.8.: Data path of compact AES-based architecture

of the data at a time. For this, the first fragment, which is as big as the memory location *data* allows, is en-/decrypted and the internal results are kept in the AES core until the host system provides the next fragment and orders the continuation. The last pass, by which the final results are generated, may be indicated by a flag in the command word.

Note that this operation is its own inverse, see Section 4.4.2. Therefore, plaintext is converted into ciphertext and vice versa.

GenerateHash This command calculates the hash value of the content of the memory location *data*. The initial value $H_0 = 2^{256} - 1$ has to be written to the associated memory location beforehand by the host system. From the same memory location the final result may be read afterwards.

Similar to the operation En-/Decrypt, the amount of data may be split into different fragments, if it is too big to completely fit into the available memory.

GenerateRandom This command produces a random 256 bit number, which is provided in the memory location *result*. It expects a 256 bit value of additional input in the memory location *add_input*. This value may be used to additionally personalize the random numbers or can be set to 0. The memory location *internal key* stores the associated part of the internal state of the random number generator, see Section 4.4.4. The internal key must be written by the host system only during the initialization.

Reseed This command is used to (re)initialize the CSRNG. For the initialization, the host system writes 0 as internal key and a seed into the respective memory loca-

7.4. Auxiliary function core

Table 7.6.: Interface memory configuration

Start address	Word length	Name	Used for En-/Decrypt	Hash	CSRNG
0x000	464	data	✓	✓	−
0x1D0	8	key	✓	−	−
0x1D8	3	nonce	✓	−	−
0x1DB	1	−	−	−	−
0x1DC	8	seed/add_input	−	−	✓
0x1E4	4	internal key	−	−	✓
0x1E8	8	result	−	−	✓
0x1F0	8	H_0/result	−	✓	−
0x1F8	8	−	−	−	−

tions. For the reinitialization only a new seed is provided, while the internal key is left unchanged. The reseed counter, which indicates after how many generated random numbers a reseed is necessary, has to be handled by the host system.

A command to the AES core is issued in form of a write access to the address 0x1000. The structure of a command word send during such a write access is depicted in Figure 7.9. Note that only the 16 most significant bits are used.

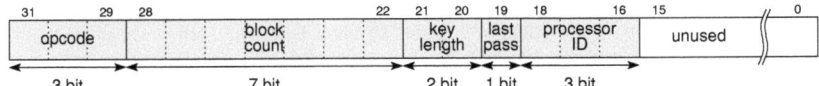

Figure 7.9.: Structure of the command word for the AES core

The field *opcode* denotes the command to be issued. The mapping from bit code to command name can be found in Table 7.7. The amount of data to operate on is given as *block count* in words with a width of 32 bit. The *key length* is provided as bit code, which is depicted in the last column of Table 7.7. The field *last pass* indicates, whether the current command is the last in a sequence working on multiple data fragments. If the data fits into a single fragment only, *last pass* is set. The *processor ID*, finally, identifies the processor, which issues the command. This is important, because only that processor, which has currently acquired the AES core, is allowed to start operations.

With a read access to the address 0x1000 the host system may read out the status of the AES core. The structure of the returned status word is depicted in Figure 7.10. Note that only the six most significant bits are actually used.

The field *status bit code* of the status word contains the current state of the AES core. Table 7.8 contains the mapping from bit code to meaning of the status. The *current processor ID* identifies that processor, which currently has acquired the AES core exclusively. This allows a processor to recognize, whether itself or another processor has a lock on the AES core.

Table 7.7.: Commands for the AES core

Opcode	Command	Allowed key-lengths	Key-length bit code
000	En-/Decrypt	128 bit	00
		192 bit	10
		256 bit	11
010	GenerateHash	256 bit	11
100	GenerateRandom	128 bit	00
101	Reseed	128 bit	00

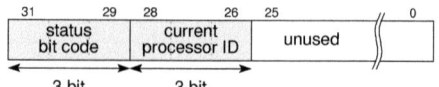

Figure 7.10.: Structure of the status word for the AES core

Algorithm 7.1 provides the general execution flow for the usage of the AES core in pseudo-code. In line 1 to 7 the processor checks, whether the core is free and, subsequently, acquires it. In line 8 to 15 the processor executes the operations, if necessary in several passes. In line 16, finally, the core is released, so it may be used by other processors. Note that in the lines 5, 10, and 16 each time the same command word[3] is send, its concrete meaning depending on the current position in the algorithm.

7.4.3. AES module

The AES module consists of the unit for the AES encryption and the unit for the key scheduler. The AES encryption unit depicted in Figure 7.11 is designed according to the design from [19]. However, the differences in functionality made two significant changes necessary. Firstly, besides the key size of 128 bit, the AES core also supports key sizes of 192 bit and 256 bit, which requires the handling of an increased number of rounds. For the realization of the hash function a block size of 256 bit[4] is required, thus, a more fine-grained access to the *folded register* is introduced. Secondly, because none of the three auxiliary functions utilizes the decryption, it is omitted, which somewhat simplifies the data path. The folded register is a customized hardware element, which implicitly executes the row shift operation of the AES algorithm. The element *SubBytes* realizes the byte substitution by exploiting two BRAMs as look-up table.

The key scheduler unit depicted in Figure 7.12 is also designed according to [19]. Again, the differences in functionality led to some structural changes. For the additional

---
[3]Of course, the bit *last pass* may be set differently, if multiple passes are required.
[4]Because of this increased block size, the AES module does not conform to the AES specification in a strict sense, but rather calculates a general Rijndael cipher.

7.4. Auxiliary function core

Table 7.8.: Meaning of the status values for the AES core

Value	Status
0x00	idle
0x01	waiting for input data from current processor
0x02	busy
0x03	waiting for continuation by same processor
0x04	waiting for release from current processor

Algorithm 7.1 Usage of the AES core
1: **repeat**
2:   **repeat**
3:     check state of the core
4:   **until** (core is *idle*)
5:   issue command word to core (as request)
6:   check current processor ID
7: **until** (*current processor ID* = own processor ID)
8: **repeat**
9:   write parameter/data into the memory of the core
10:   issue command word to the core (as command)
11:   **repeat**
12:     check state of the core
13:   **until** (core is *waiting for continuation by same processor*)
14:   read result from memory of the core
15: **until** (no additional pass needed)
16: issue command word to core (to free core)

key length of 256 bit, the AES algorithm exhibits an anomaly in its flow, see [83]. For this, a data path is required bypassing the XOR and the operation *Rotate Word*. The *shift register* had to be extended to depths 5 and 7 to also handle the key-lengths of 192 bit and 256 bit, respectively. Generally, shift registers in the AES core are FIFO-like structures with a word-widths of 32 bit, where the number of words, which may be stored, is denoted depth. Finally, because the key schedule is – in contrast to the design in [19] – generated concurrently, *SubBytes* of the encrypt unit may not be reused and two more BRAMs are required as look-up table for the *SubBytes* operation of the key scheduler unit.

7.4.4. Auxiliary unit for the counter-mode encryption

The auxiliary unit for counter-mode encryption is depicted in Figure 7.13. The nonce-sequence to be encrypted consists of the 3-word nonce from memory concatenated with the 32-bit value in the *counter register*, which is set to 1 at the beginning of each en-/decryption. The key for the encryption is expected at the associated location in

Chapter 7. Prototype implementation

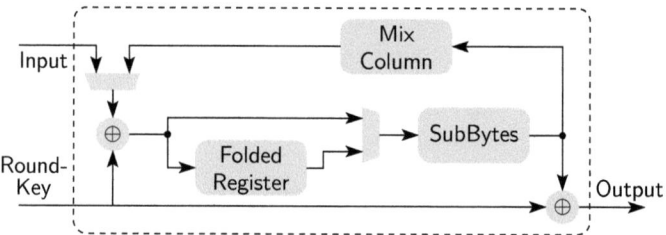

Figure 7.11.: Structure of AES encryption unit

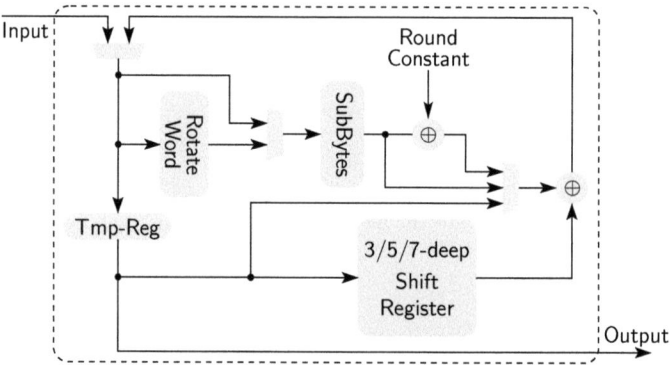

Figure 7.12.: Structure of AES key scheduler unit

memory.

After the current nonce value is fed into the encryption module and latter one is working, the next 128 bit block of plain-/ciphertext is loaded into the shift register, while its current content is XORed with the previous encryption result and, subsequently, stored in memory. In this process, the newly generated data block is written over the original one.

7.4.5. Auxiliary unit for the hash function

The main element of the auxiliary unit for the hash function, which is depicted in Figure 7.14, is a *shift register* with a depth of 8. The hashing operation starts with reading the 256 bit block at the memory location H_0 provided by the host system into the shift register. For each block of the data to hash, the intermediate hash value H_i is written into this same memory location, thus, the previous value is always substituted by the current one. At the end of the computation the final value H is computed according to Equation (4.1c).

7.4. Auxiliary function core

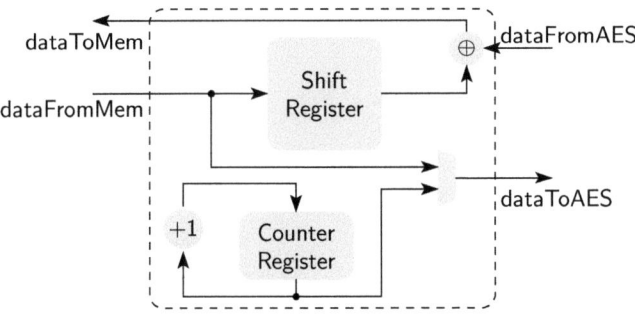

Figure 7.13.: Auxiliary unit for counter-mode encryption

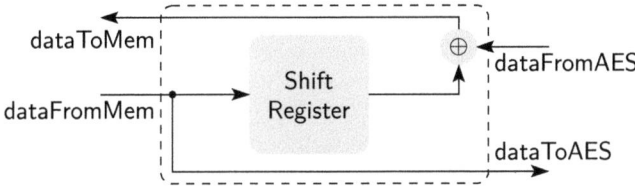

Figure 7.14.: Auxiliary unit for hash function

7.4.6. Auxiliary unit for the random number generator

The auxiliary unit for the cryptographically secure random number generator (CSRNG) is depicted in Figure 7.15. The *shift register* has a depth of 8 and is used to store temporary values. The 128-bit value V, which is part of the internal state, is stored in the *value register* and is increased during every update operation on the internal state. The AES module is used with 128 bit for both the key-length and the block-length. According to the standard from [6], this results in an output block-length of 256 bit. The standard leaves some additional implementation options. Because of the goal of compactness, the less complicated variants were chosen. An exception is the input value *additional_info*, which is included, because this results in less exceptions in the computational flow.

7.4.7. Performance

The performance figures for the AES core from [61] are derived from an implementation on the XUPV2P board. Table 7.9 provides the slice counts required by the different units of the AES core. In total, 916 slices and 5 BRAMs are needed. 1 BRAM is used as interface memory and 4 as look-up tables in the encryption and key scheduler unit. Note that compared to the design from [19] the AES module of the AES core is 63 slices larger, because it needs to be able to operate on additional key and block lengths.

93

Chapter 7. Prototype implementation

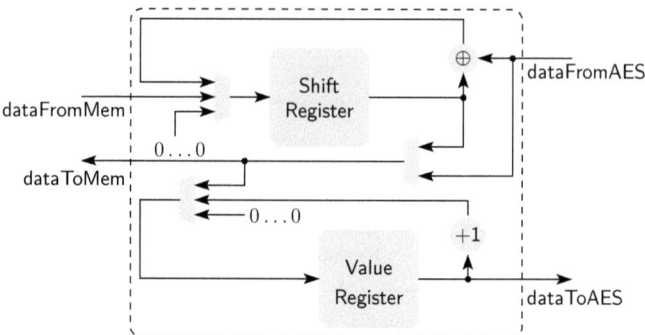

Figure 7.15.: Auxiliary unit for the CSRNG

Table 7.9.: Resource usage for each unit

Unit	#slices
Encryption unit	164
Key scheduler unit	121
Counter-mode unit	129
Hash unit	81
CSRNG unit	368
Controller	50
Bus logic	3
Sum	**916**

The amount of required clock cycles for the supported functions is depicted in Table 7.10, where N denotes the number of blocks.

Table 7.11, finally, shows the throughput figures for the different functions assuming a clock frequency of 100MHz. The performance is adequate to prevent the auxiliary functions from becoming the bottleneck for the computation of a scheme on the prototype implementation of the co-processor.

7.5. MicroBlaze soft-cores processors

The MicroBlaze soft-core processors are utilized by the central core to compute the cryptographic schemes and, in turn, exploit the ModArith and AES core for this. The hardware view for the interfaces to these two cores was already illustrated above, thus, the associated low level software, i.e., the drivers, is explained in the following.

Furthermore, this section presents details on the structure of the software for the soft-cores. Besides the general execution flow this includes a list and description of the

Table 7.10.: Clock cycles needed for number of blocks N

Operation	Key size	Clock cycles
Counter-mode de-/encryption	128 bit	$45 \cdot N$
	192 bit	$53 \cdot N$
	256 bit	$61 \cdot N$
CSRNG	128 bit	188
CSRNG Reseed	128 bit	96
AES Hash	256 bit	$121 \cdot (N+1)$

Table 7.11.: Throughput for the different operations

Operation	Key size	Throughput
Counter-mode de-/encryption	128 bit	284.4 Mbps
	192 bit	241.5 Mbps
	256 bit	209.8 Mbps
CSRNG	128 bit	136.2 Mbps
AES Hash	256 bit	211.5 Mbps

supported operations and of the chosen algorithm variants for the different schemes and their realization.

7.5.1. Driver for the ModArith core

The driver for the ModArith core encapsulates the actual access to the FSL for the application code realizing the scheme execution. The available functions mirror closely the available access types described in Section 7.3.1. There are, however, additional functions performing the actual waiting for one or both multipliers to finish execution. Note that this realization of the waiting for the completion of modular operations as part of the FSL significantly increases the readability and transparency of the code for the cryptographic schemes.

ModArith_Read This function expects an address as parameter and returns the value of the word stored at this address in memory bank A of the ModArith core, see Section 7.3.2.

ModArith_Write This function expects an address and a 32-bit word as parameters and writes the value of the word at the given address into the memory of the ModArith core.

ModArith_GetStatus This function returns the status word of the ModArith core.

ModArith_Op This function expects the *opcode* and the addresses *destination*, *source1*, *source2*, and *modulus* for a command to the ModArith core. It issues the command and returns after the completion of the modular operation or immediately, if a multiplication was started.

ModArith_Wait_A This function may be utilized to delay execution until the multiplier ModMultA is finished, as it does not return before this time. Internally, it uses the command GetStatus with the bit *waitA* set.

ModArith_Wait_B This function may be utilized to delay execution until the multiplier ModMultB is finished, as it does not return before this time. Internally, it uses the command GetStatus with the bit *waitB* set.

ModArith_Wait_AB This function may be utilized to delay execution until both multipliers are finished, as it does not return before this time. Internally, it uses the command GetStatus with the bits *waitA* and *waitB* set.

7.5.2. Driver for the AES core

The software interface for the AES core provides a function for each of the four commands. These use some low-level driver functions like `requestCore` and `releaseCore` for the actual access of the AES core. Thus, the software executing the schemes does not need to operate on the AES core directly, but via one of the following four functions, which provide a more convenient interface.

AesCounterCrypt This function expects the data to be en-/decrypted and its length as parameter and returns the en-/decrypted data. If the amount of data is too large to be en-/decrypted in one pass, multiple passes are executed on the AES core as described in Section 7.4.2.

AesHash This function expects the data to be hashed and its length as parameter and returns the calculated hash value. If the amount of data is too large to be hashed in one pass, multiple passes are executed on the AES core as described in Section 7.4.2.

AesGetRnd This function has no parameters and orders the AES core to generate a new random number. The resulting 256-bit value may be read afterwards from the memory location named `aesRnd`.

AesInitRnd This function expects the seed as parameter and (re)initializes the random number generator as described in Section 7.4.2.

7.5.3. Software structure and interface

This section presents the coarse-grained structure of the software on the MicroBlaze processors. Its execution starts with the initialization of the shared memory. This is followed by a handshake with the PowerPC providing each MicroBlaze core with its processor ID. Finally, the AES core is initialized and the soft-cores start waiting for instructions. This waiting is realized in a *busy waiting* manner by the function `Dispatch`. Note that a detailed description of the handshake and the inter-processor communication between the MicroBlaze processors and the PowerPC is deferred to Section 7.7.

The function `Dispatch` is the central function of the scheme controllers and is responsible for receiving the instructions from the central core and for supervising their execution. After a command is received, the associated operation is executed. When it is completed, the final results are written into the shared memory. This is indicated to the central core, which, in turn, acknowledges the reception. Finally, the soft-core starts again waiting for new instructions. The commands supported by the scheme controller are as follows.

NOP This command results in no operation. In a strict sense, it is not a command, but a marker telling the MicroBlaze processor that no command was issued.

RSA_SET_PARAMETERS This command instructs the MicroBlaze processor to load new RSA parameters from the shared memory area into the memory of the ModArith core. This command must precede every RSA scheme following an ECC or PBC operation and every RSA operation using a new parameter set.

RSA_RSASSA_SIGN This command computes the signature of an amount of data using the previously set RSA parameters following the RSASSA standard. The data is expected in the corresponding location in the shared memory.

RSA_RSASSA_VERIFY This command verifies a signature for an amount of data using the previously set RSA parameters following the RSASSA standard. The data and the associated signature are expected in the corresponding locations in the shared memory.

RSA_RSAES_ENCRYPT This command encrypts an amount of data using the previously set RSA parameters following the RSAES standard. The data is expected in the corresponding location in the shared memory.

RSA_RSAES_DECRYPT This command decrypts an amount of data using the previously set RSA parameters following the RSAES standard. The data is expected in the corresponding location in the shared memory.

ECC_SET_PARAMETERS This command instructs the soft-core to load new ECC domain parameters from the shared memory area into the memory of the ModArith core. It must precede every ECC scheme following an RSA or PBC operation and every ECC operation over a new set of domain parameters. Note that this instruction also calculates the value of the Weierstraß-coefficient $a = q - 3$.

ECC_KEY_GENERATE Using the current ECC domains parameters, this command generates a new key pair as described in Section 4.1.2. For this, the scheme controller creates a random number $x \in [0, n-1]$ as private key and computes the point multiplication $Q = xG$ as public key.

ECC_KEY_VALIDATE This command may be used to validate an ECC key. This is done according to [39, Algorithm 4.25], however, without checking $nQ = \infty$, because this is very costly computation-wise and it is not possible to import keys from the outside in the prototype implementation.

ECC_ECDSA_SIGN This command computes the signature of an amount of data using the previously set ECC domain parameters following the ECDSA standard. The data is expected in the corresponding location in the shared memory.

ECC_ECDSA_VERIFY This command verifies a signature for an amount of data using the previously set ECC domain parameters following the ECDSA standard. The data and the associated signature are expected in the corresponding locations in the shared memory.

ECC_ECIES_ENCRYPT This command encrypts an amount of data using the previously set ECC domain parameters following the ECIES standard. The data is expected in the corresponding location in the shared memory.

ECC_ECIES_DECRYPT This command decrypts an amount of data using the previously set ECC domain parameters following the ECIES standard. The data is expected in the corresponding location in the shared memory.

PBC_KEY_GENERATE Using the current PBC domain parameters, this command generates a new key pair as described in Section 4.1.3. For this, the scheme controller creates a random number $x \in \mathbb{GF}(q)$ as private key and computes the point multiplication $Q = xG$ as public key.

PBC_BLS_SIGN This command computes the signature of an amount of data using the previously set PBC domain parameters according to the BLS signature generation. The data is expected in the corresponding location in the shared memory.

PBC_BLS_VERIFY This command verifies a signature for an amount of data using the previously set PBC domain parameters according to the BLS signature verification. The data and the associated signature are expected in the corresponding locations in the shared memory.

Note that there is no command *PBC_SET_PARAMETERS*, because the prototype realization reuses the command *ECC_SET_PARAMETERS* for this task. This is possible, because PBC has nearly the same values in its parameter set: The Weierstraß-coefficients a and b are not used, because their values are coded directly into the algorithm of the pairing. Only the cofactor h is additionally needed for PBC, but just in the software of the scheme controller, which may read it directly from the shared memory. Thus, it was sufficient to introduce a new memory configuration layout for PBC.

The command *RSA_KEY_GENERATE* does not exists, because the key generation for RSA may not be computed using the Montgomery multiplication realized in the ModArith core. For the key generation $d \equiv e^{-1} \mod ((p-1)(q-1))$ must be calculated. However, both $(p-1)$ and $(q-1)$ are even, resulting in the modulus $(p-1)(q-1)$ also being even. For the Montgomery multiplication the modulus and R have to be relatively prime, which is then not the case anymore.

7.5.4. Realization details for RSA

This section explains some implementation details of the important algorithms used for RSA. This is mainly the modular exponentiation and the basic decryption operation. Latter one exploits the optimization using the Chinese Remainder Theorem. Note that the modular exponentiation is also needed for algorithms in ECC and PBC.

Algorithm for modular exponentiation

The modular exponentiation is needed for RSA as cryptographic main operation. It is realized using the Montgomery Powering Ladder, see Algorithm 4.11. Compared to a simple "Square and Multiply" algorithm, it allows the exploitation of both modular multiplier instances. For this, the parallel multiplications are mapped to the parallel multipliers. Furthermore, the Montgomery Powering Ladder provides a better protection against side channel attacks because of its uniform execution flow. However, it is noteworthy that in each step of the loop a copy operation of an intermediate result from one memory bank into the other is necessary. The direction depends on whether the if- or the else-branch is executed. The modular exponentiation is also utilized in ECC and PBC, e.g., for modular inversion and modular square root.

Algorithm for encryption

As described in Chapter 4, the basic encryption operation for RSA consists of the simple modular exponentiation:
$$m = c^e \mod n$$

Algorithm for decryption exploiting the Chinese Remainder Theorem

The fact that the RSA modulus n is a product of the two prime numbers p and q may be utilized to increase the efficiency of the decryption operation by exploiting the Chinese Remainder Theorem (CRT), see Section 3.2.3. Note that this approach is not possible for the encryption operation, because p and q must not be part of the public key.

Thus, as stated in [74] the decryption operation
$$c = m^d \mod n$$

Chapter 7. Prototype implementation

may be substituted by the following equations.

$$c_p = (m \mod p)^{d \mod (p-1)} \mod p$$
$$c_q = (m \mod q)^{d \mod (q-1)} \mod q$$
$$c = c_q + ((c_p - c_q) \cdot (q^{-1} \mod p) \mod p) \cdot q$$

The values $d \mod (p-1)$, $d \mod (q-1)$, and $q^{-1} \mod p$ are precomputed and part of the extended private key, see Section 4.1.1. The efficiency increase stems mainly from the shorter exponentiations, which exhibit exponents of about half the bit-length and also consist of modular multiplications with a modulus of about half the bit-length. Thus, they require less multiplications, which are about a quarter as costly.

The recombination in the last step is derived from Garner's algorithm. This algorithm, however, requires non-modular operations, which are not provided by the ModArith core. Fortunately, the input values of these calculations have only half the bit-length of n. Thus, because the length of the final results does not exceed

$$(2^{\frac{m}{2}} - 1) + (2^{\frac{m}{2}} - 1) \cdot (2^{\frac{m}{2}} - 1) =$$
$$(2^{\frac{m}{2}} - 1) + (2^{\frac{m}{2}} \cdot (2^{\frac{m}{2}} - 1) - 2 \cdot (2^{\frac{m}{2}} - 1) + 1) =$$
$$2^m - 2^{\frac{m}{2}} < 2^m - 1$$

bits in the worst case, where m is the bit-length of n, it is possible to use a Montgomery multiplication with $2^m - 1$ as modulus. The R associated with this modulus is equal to 1 making transformations to and from the Montgomery space unnecessary. However, during the calculations before this final recombination, which are executed modulo p or q, respectively, several transformations to and from the Montgomery space are needed.

7.5.5. Realization details for ECC

In comparison to RSA an additional abstraction level is needed for ECC, which contains point addition and doubling. These are utilized in the point multiplication, which is the cryptographic main operation of ECC. To exploit parallel multipliers efficiently during the relatively complex point addition and doubling, a design space exploration was done finding feasible schedules. Finally, the conversion back to affine coordinates requires a modular inversion, which, however, is implemented straight forward.

Point multiplication

For the point multiplication the prototype implementation exploits the Montgomery Powering Ladder, see Algorithm 4.11. Although this is not as efficient as a simple "Double and Add" algorithm, because it requires more point additions, it was still chosen, because it exhibits an uniform execution flow and, thus, provides some protection against side channel attacks.

Modular Inversion

The modular inversion is calculated according to Fermat's Little Theorem, thus, it is basically a modular exponentiation, which was explained in Section 7.5.4. Thus, both parallel multiplier instances of each ModArith core are exploited.

Multiplier mapping for point addition and doubling

The algorithms for point addition and doubling from Section 3.3 exhibit multiple modular operations, which somehow have to be mapped to the available hardware modules of the ModArith cores without violating any data dependencies. Thus, feasible schedules have to be generated, which also keep the time small, during which the multipliers stay unused. Because this problem is NP-hard – i.e., in general, it is not easy to find a (nearly) optimal solution – an automated approach is utilized in this work.

For this, the high-level synthesis tool hCDM from [55, 54, 49] was utilized. By using a genetic algorithm, this tool generates optimized realizations for embedded systems consisting of an allocation of resources, of a binding of tasks to allocated resources, and of a schedule deciding the execution order of the tasks. As a specialty, the optimization of the hCDM-tool can be guided by multiple design criteria. For the prototype implementation mainly the scheduling aspect of the hCDM-tool was used.

Figure 7.16 shows the basic work-flow of the hCDM-tool. As input the tool is given information about tasks, resources, data dependencies, and which task may be executed on which resource. The *task graph* contains the description of the tasks and their data dependencies. The *resource graph* comprises the specification about the resources including which tasks may be executed on each of them in which estimated time. Starting from these information, a genetic algorithm is used to generate feasible allocations, bindings, and schedules.

Genetic algorithms are heuristic search algorithms based on the theory of evolution. They employ natural selection to incrementally increase the quality of the solutions, which are also called *individuals*. As depicted in Figure 7.17, the algorithm starts with the *initialization* function generating a random set of individuals called a *generation*. Subsequently, each individual of this first generation is then assigned a score value by the *evaluation* function according to the criteria chosen by the designer. In the next step the *selection* function is used to pick individuals with high score values as foundation for the next generation. With a low probability these solutions are then slightly modified by the *mutation* function. The next generation is then created by the *crossover* function, which combines the properties of two or more selected individuals to produce offspring. Finally, this cycle starts again with the evaluation step until a certain number of generations or a certain score level is reached.

Genetic algorithms are well-suited to solve complex problems, as they can search through large search spaces while avoiding local optima. For this, they rely mainly on the quality of the solution representation and of the evaluation, crossover, and mutation function. These are also the central parts, which have to be implemented to solve a problem using a genetic algorithm.

Chapter 7. Prototype implementation

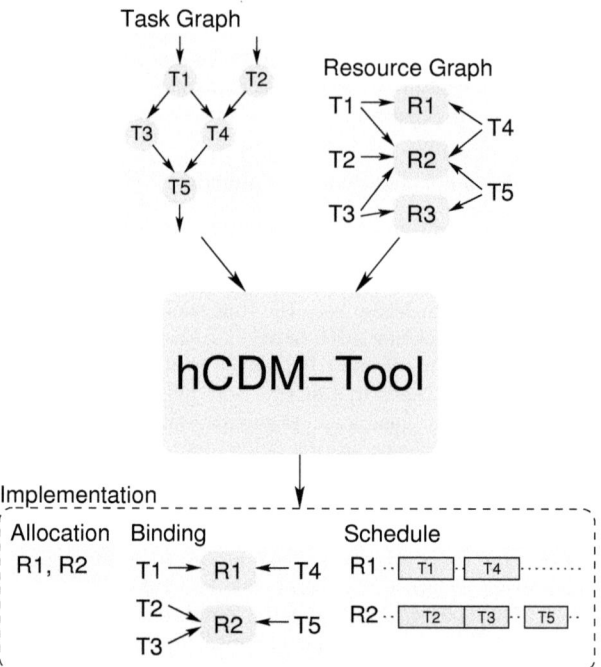

Figure 7.16.: Outline of the work-flow of the hCDM-tool

In Table 7.12 the representation of a solution in hCDM is depicted. The allocation consists of a subset of the available resources, thus, an implementation does not have to contain all resources. The binding assigns each task to that one of the chosen resources it is executed on. The chronological order of the tasks, finally, is stored in the schedule, which is realized by assigning each task an unique priority.

As an example, the mutation function is depicted in the last row of Table 7.12. For the mutation of the allocation, one resource is randomly removed. If this leads to an allocation, which does not contain a possible resource for each task, the allocation is repaired by randomly adding resources for the tasks in question. For the mutation of the binding, each task is assigned a different resource out of the current allocation, if possible. For the mutation of the schedule, the priorities of two randomly selected tasks are exchanged.

The score values are given by the evaluation function according to the Pareto-optimality of a solution. Therefore, the score of a solution quantifies the amount of individuals dominated by the evaluated solution. In this context, a solution dominates another one, if it features equal or better values in all criteria. Consequently, the hCDM-tool results

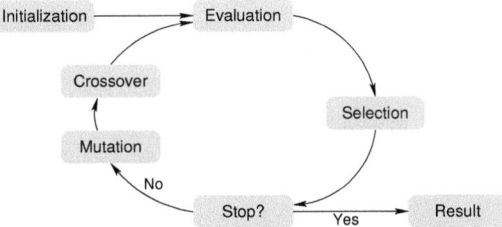

Figure 7.17.: Outline of a genetic algorithm

Table 7.12.: Representation of an individual

	Allocation	Binding	Schedule
Purpose	Determine set of resources	Assign a resource to each task	Assign a priority to each task
Example	R1, R3, ...	(T1, R3), (T2, R1), ..., (Tn, R5)	(T1, 4), (T2, n), ..., (Tn, 1)
Mutation operation	Remove/add resources	Select new resource from allocation	Exchange priorities

in a set of Pareto-optimal individuals and the designer may choose that one, which fits the problem best.

The hCDM-tool was used to create feasible schedules for point addition and doubling on the ModArith core. Three resources representing the two modular multipliers and the remaining arithmetic, timing estimates for the different modular operations, and the data flow graphs were fed into the tool. However, possible bindings for the multiplications were restricted to enforce the assignment of subsequent multiplications onto the same multiplier instance. This results in the minimization of the required copying as described in Section 6.2.2.

The algorithms for point addition and doubling utilized in the prototype implementation were presented in Section 3.3, see Algorithm 3.7 and Algorithm 3.8. The data flow graphs derived from these algorithms are depicted in Figure 7.18(a) and Figure 7.18(b), respectively. Note that the use of a single value at both inputs of an operation is displayed as parallel arrows.

Multiplications are indicated by the light and dark gray symbols and the color shows, on which of the parallel multipliers the particular multiplication is calculated. This is important, as the execution of subsequent multiplications on the same instance reduces the need for copying. For example, the multiplications *SQR1* and *MULT2* in Figure 7.18(a) are executed on the multiplier *ModMultA*, while *SQR5* is executed on the multiplier *ModMultB*.

Figure 7.19 shows the schedules for point addition generated with the hCDM-tool.

Chapter 7. Prototype implementation

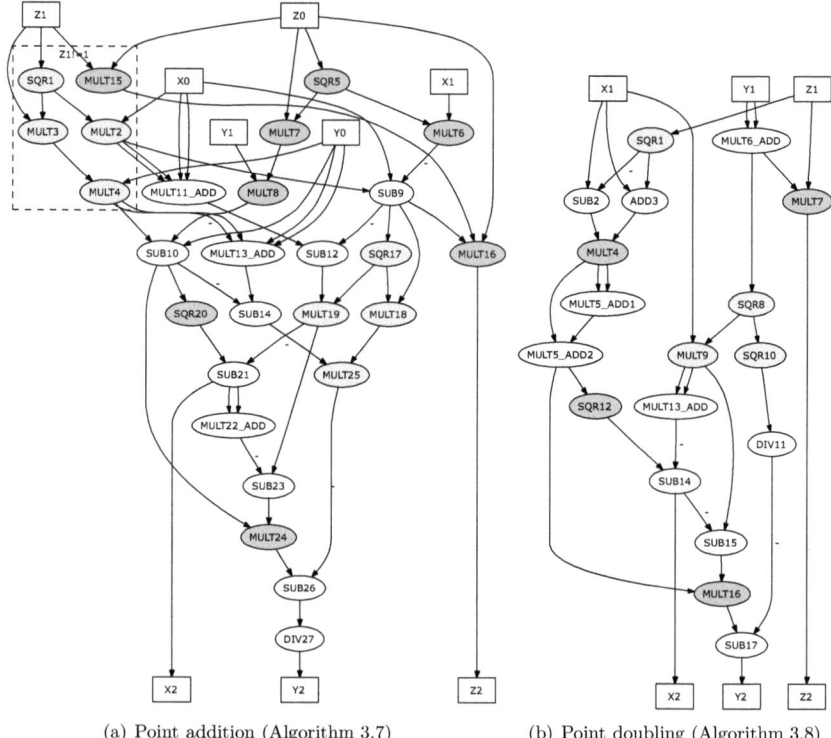

(a) Point addition (Algorithm 3.7) (b) Point doubling (Algorithm 3.8)

Figure 7.18.: Data flow graphs for point addition and doubling

Figure 7.19(a) depicts the general case, while the case $z_1 = 1$ may be seen in Figure 7.19(b). Note that actually $z_1 = R$ is checked, because the operations are calculated in the Montgomery space, where R is the multiplicative neutral element.

Figure 7.20 shows the corresponding schedule for point doubling.

7.5.6. Realization details for PBC

For the additional implementation of PBC besides ECC and RSA, several new functions were needed, whose code was modeled according to that from the PBC Library, see [68]. Nearly all new functions are needed for the actual pairing, except for the hash-to-point operation.

The functions were realized relatively straight forward starting from their description as found in Section 3.4.4 for the operations in the extension field and Section 4.4.6

7.5. MicroBlaze soft-cores processors

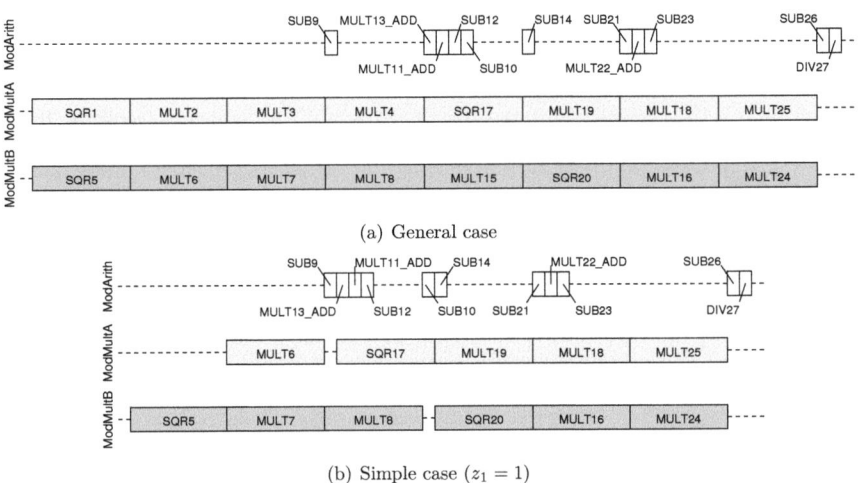

Figure 7.19.: Schedules for point addition executed on two multipliers

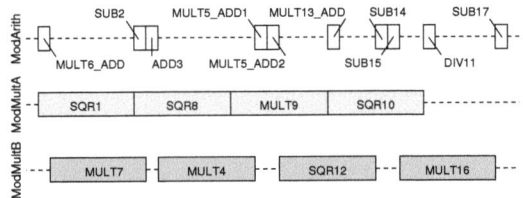

Figure 7.20.: Schedule for point doubling executed on two multipliers

for hash-to-point. Although schedules supporting two parallel multipliers had to be generated for each function, the major effort lay in the creation of correct code, which required extensive debugging. This is because the functions are usually short enough to allow finding good schedules by hand.

An exception is the point doubling operation, which had to be realized again for PBC, because the Weierstraß-quotients are different than in the ECC realization. As described in Section 3.4.3 the Weierstraß-quotients were set to $a = 1$ and $b = 0$ for PBC, while a was set to -3 for ECC. The schedule for point doubling for PBC was generated using the same approach as for ECC using the hCDM-tool.

105

Chapter 7. Prototype implementation

7.6. Central core

According to the proposed architecture, the central core is responsible for the communication with the host server and the supervision of the scheme controllers. In the prototype implementation, however, former functionality is incorporated only rudimentarily. The program for the PowerPC contains only code for testing the execution of the different schemes on the MicroBlaze processors. Because of the proof-of-concept nature of the prototype a true two-way communication allowing the host server to issue requests was not implemented. Instead, only the results of the tests of the scheme controllers are send to the host system via the UART-interface.

Because of its task of testing the scheme executions, the software for the PowerPC contains mainly two types of functions: Those for checking correctness of the calculations and those for measuring their execution time. The remaining functions mostly provide functionality like initialization or pretty printing. Furthermore, for the testing of the scheme controllers the code of the central core contains the parameter sets introduced in Section 7.1.

The correctness of the realizations of the supported schemes is tested by, subsequently, executing the complementary operations with some test data and checking, whether the final result is equal to the original test data. For this, the test data is encrypted or signed and the intermediate result of this function is then decrypted or verified, respectively. If the result of the last operation is equal to the original test data, the implementation of the scheme works correctly. Note that for ECC and PBC a new key is generated before each encryption and signing operation, respectively, to introduce an element of randomness. This is not possible for RSA, as described in Section 4.1.1.

For the measurement of the execution time, each scheme is executed 2000 times with some test data. In this case, however, it is not checked, whether the result of the operation is correct. To gain the average execution time of a single operation, the overall execution time is divided by 2000. Note that this value does not only contain the raw calculation time, but also the time needed for the communication between the cores.

7.7. Inter-processor communication

The communication between the MicroBlaze processors and the PowerPC processor is accomplished using the shared memory. Basically, the behavior to send some information is the same for both parties. The data acting as parameters for an instruction or as return values is written into predetermined memory locations. To actually trigger the communication, a bit code signifying the type of the communication is written to another memory location, which is repeatedly read by the receiving party in a *busy waiting* manner.

Busy waiting is usually avoided, because it wastes processor cycles, which could be used for useful computations. Instead, an interrupt approach may be used, in which the receiving party is notified about the message by means of an interrupt. After this, the receiver copies the data to its memory, acknowledges the reception, and continues the execution at that point of execution, at which it was interrupted.

In the prototype implementation, this approach was not adopted, because the processor, which is busy waiting for some information, usually has nothing else to do, thus, no cycles are wasted. This is especially true, for the MicroBlaze processors, whose only task is the execution of scheme calculations. The PowerPC, on the other hand, has to communicate with multiple soft-cores and the host system. However, it is significantly faster than the soft-cores and has a significantly smaller work load. Therefore, it is waiting most of the time. Finally, because the operations, which are required to acknowledge a scheme result and to issue the next one, are relatively small and because of the proof-of-concept nature of the prototype, it was decided to accept this small delay.

Although the PowerPC could theoretically access the complete data memories of the MicroBlaze processors, only a part of each is utilized as shared memory. The remainder is used as normal data memory for the soft-cores. This is accomplished by instructing the linker to leave some area unoccupied. Thus, the code of both processor types has complete control over it. Therefore, it is also not initialized by compiler generated code, but this is instead performed by the MicroBlaze processors, which fill this area with 0 at start up time.

As depicted in Figure 7.21, this initialization is followed by a handshake with the PowerPC. This handshake provides each soft core with an unique processor ID and guarantees the PowerPC that the MicroBlaze processors have entered the busy waiting state, thus, commands to compute cryptographic schemes may be issued.

The flow of the inter-processor communication is depicted in Figure 7.22. As part of the initialization described above, the MicroBlaze processor sets the memory locations COMMAND and RESULT to their neutral values. In this context, COMMAND denotes the location, into which the PowerPC may write commands for the soft-core. RESULT may be used by the scheme controller to send replies for the central core. After this, the MicroBlaze processor starts busy waiting for commands from the PowerPC. In contrast, latter one interprets the setting of the neutral values as sign that the soft-core is ready to receive commands and starts executing its own program.

The basic flow of one scheme execution is as follows: The PowerPC writes a new opcode distinct from NOP, see Section 7.5.3, into COMMAND. This is observed by the MicroBlaze processor, which subsequently starts executing the desired scheme. During this time the central core is busy waiting for the reply from the scheme controller. This reply – either **SUCCESS** or **ERROR** – is written into RESULT by the soft-core after the completion of the scheme. After the PowerPC receives the reply, it acknowledges it by setting both memory locations to their neutral values and continues with its program. The soft-core, in turn, interprets this acknowledgment as signal to start busy waiting for new commands again.

The memory locations COMMAND and RESULT are both part of the second memory location of the shared memory, see Table 7.13. This location has a length of 4 bytes and its least significant byte is used by the PowerPC as COMMAND. The most significant nibble of this location is utilized as RESULT.

The complete configuration of the shared memory is depicted in Table 7.13. The first

Chapter 7. Prototype implementation

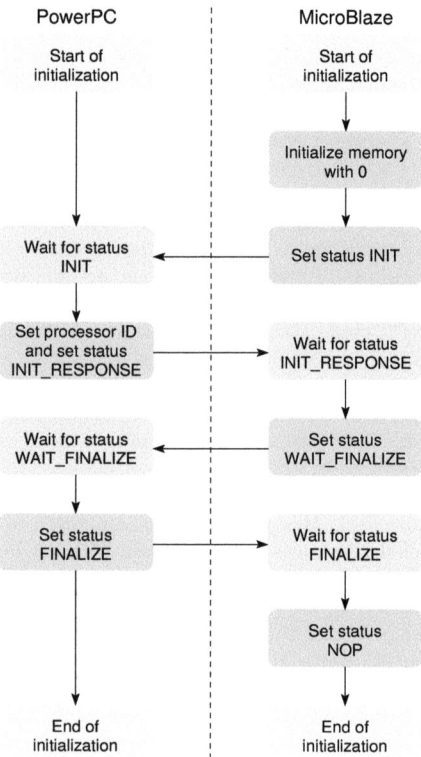

Figure 7.21.: Initialization of the shared memory

location contains the processor ID, which is set during start up. The second location is utilized for the communication between the processors, as described above. The third location is used to transfer the domain parameters for either RSA or ECC schemes. Debug messages from the MicroBlaze processors may be written to the fourth location. They are read by the PowerPC, whenever is notified about their presence using a special value in the location RETURN. Then, the PowerPC sends the message on to the host system via the UART interface. The message to be de-/encrypted or signed/verified is conveyed in the fifth location, accompanied by its length in the sixth location. The last memory location is utilized for parameters/replies only needed for the particular type of the currently given command. For example, the private key is written in here by the PowerPC for an ECDSA sign command and the MicroBlaze returns the computed signature in this location as well.

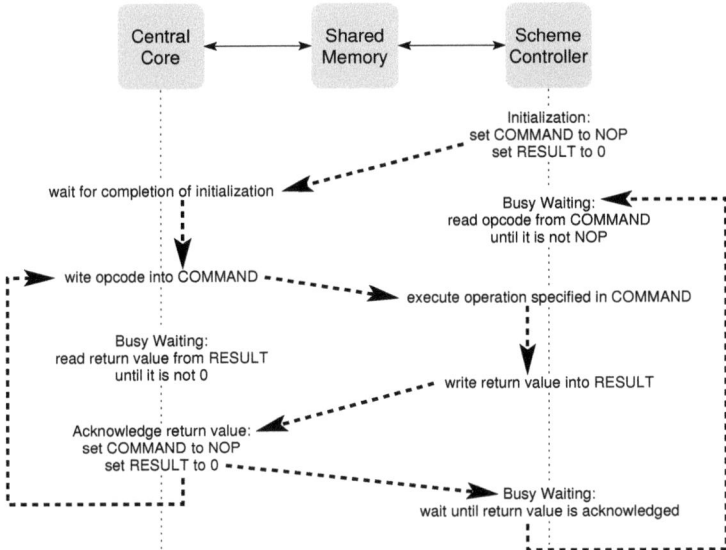

Figure 7.22.: Visualization of the inter-processor communication

7.8. Example: RSA encryption

In the following, the execution of an encryption using the RSAES-OAEP scheme is presented in more detail as an example. The other schemes are executed similarly according to the respective scheme algorithms given in Chapter 4.

- To execute an RSA encryption, the PowerPC issues the command RSA_RSAES_-ENCRYPT to a MicroBlaze processor by, first, writing the message M and, then, the command into the respective locations in the shared memory, see Table 7.13.

- The function Dispatch of the MicroBlaze receives this command and first checks the length of M. If it is too long, the result ERROR is written into the shared memory and the MicroBlaze starts busy waiting for the acknowledgment from the PowerPC.

- If the message M is not too long, the function RSAES_OAEP_Encryption is executed. It is given as parameters the message M, the label L, which is the empty bit string, the bit-width, the modulus n, and the constants R and n' for the Montgomery multiplication. Latter three values must have been set beforehand by issuing the command RSA_SET_PARAMETERS.

Chapter 7. Prototype implementation

Table 7.13.: Configuration of the shared memory

Length	Content
1 Byte	Processor ID
4 Byte	COMMAND for/RESULT from soft-core
2512 Byte	Parameters for RSA or ECC
64 Byte	Memory for debug messages
1024 Byte	Message
4 Byte	Message length
768 Byte	Additional parameters/replies

- The function RSAES_OAEP_Encryption starts with creating $lHash$ by hashing the label L. Then the OAEP encoding is executed according to Figure 4.3:

  1. The concatenated value $DB = lHash||000\ldots01||M$ is build up.
  2. A random number *seed* is generated.
  3. Both these values are combined using the function MGF and the XOR-operation resulting in the message representative m.

- After the OAEP encoding is finished, the function RSAEncrypt is called with n, R, n', and m as parameters. It calculates the basic RSA encryption operation $c = m^e \mod n$ and writes the resulting chipertext c directly into the shared memory. Note that the public exponent $e = 2^{16}+1$ was set by the prior execution of the command RSA_SET_PARAMETERS, too.

- This ends the functions RSAEncrypt and RSAES_OAEP_Encryption and the function Dispatch writes the result SUCCESS into the shared memory. Then, it starts busy waiting for the acknowledgment from the PowerPC.

Therefore, for the PowerPC the execution of the command RSA_RSAES_ENCRYPT results either in the response ERROR or SUCCESS. In former case, the message was too long and could not be encrypted. In latter case, the encryption was computed and the resulting ciphertext c may be found in the last location of the shared memory, where it was written to by the function RSAEncrypt.

Chapter 8.
Results

This chapter presents the results of the prototype implementation introduced in the previous chapter. Because the architecture allows a design space with different degrees of parallelization, i.e., different amounts of pipeline stages and scheme controllers, four different variants were instantiated on the Virtex-II Pro FPGA. The resulting resource and timing figures are presented below. This is followed be a comparison with designs from literature.

Note that an earlier version of this prototype implementation was presented in [62]. However, the design variants introduced in this work exhibit an optimized modular multiplication and an improved program for the central core leading to better timing values and lower resource usages.

8.1. Resource usage

The proposed co-processor architecture was instantiated in four different configurations. The resource usage figures of these configurations are depicted in Table 8.1 together with their respective number of scheme controllers and pipeline stages.

Table 8.1.: System resource usage

Variant name	#Scheme controllers	#Pipeline stages	#Logic cells	#BRAMs
4SC2ST	4	2	26344	117
3SC3ST	3	3	24142	105
3SC4ST	3	4	23666	105
2SC6ST	2	6	21818	61

The different design variants are denoted $xSCyST$, where x means the number of scheme controllers and y stands for the amount of pipeline stages. For four and three scheme controllers the synthesis of more than two and four stages, respectively, did not succeed. It is likely that seven or more stages would have been possible for the variant with two scheme controllers. However, because of the fact that the number of words must be at least the double of the stage count, this would have prohibited further bit-widths for ECC. The usage of six stages already prohibits the computation with a bit-width of 160 and, thus, timing values for this case were not generated.

All four design variants were operated with a clock cycle frequency of 100MHz. The amount of slices required for each design variant is half the number of *logic cell*. Those are provided in the tables instead of slices to ease the comparison in Section 8.4.

Note that the design 3SC4ST requires less resource than 3SC3ST, although it features more stages. This is, because the synthesis process is somewhat chaotic: Small changes may have larger consequences. Thus, a small optimization may result in a significantly larger design. Thus, the particular resource usage relation of 3SC3ST and 3SC4ST of this work is valid only for these concrete design variants. For the slightly less optimized design variants from [62], 3SC4ST needs more resources than 3SC3ST.

Table 8.2 depicts the resource usage of a single ModArith core. The first column refers to the respective design variant, which determines the number of stages. The remaining columns contain the required amounts of logic cells, dedicated word multipliers, and block RAMs, respectively.

Table 8.2.: Resource usage of a single ModArith core

Variant	#Logic cells	#Word multipliers	#BRAMs
4SC2ST	3524	4	4
3SC3ST	4406	6	4
3SC4ST	5292	8	4
2SC6ST	7168	12	4

Thus, it can be seen that for 2SC6ST the ModArith cores require the majority of the instantiated resources, while for 4SC2ST the ModArith cores take up less than half of the used logic cells. The other design variants are somewhere between these two extremes. Note that these values will be interesting for the comparisons later on, because most realizations from literature only comprise a module for the modular multiplier or modular arithmetic, respectively.

8.2. Complete scheme operations

This section presents the timing figures gained from the four design variants of the prototype implementation. Because the aim of the proposed co-processor architecture is the calculation of complete cryptographic schemes, their execution time is measured by the central core. Thus, the values also contain the time needed for communication via the shared memory and the execution of the auxiliary functions. However, latter time is not that significant, as the messages to be operated on were kept very short, i.e., only strings with around 30 characters.

The timing figures are given as *core latency* and *total operations per second*. Both values were gained by taking the average over 2000 scheme operations on each scheme controller. The core latency denotes the average time one scheme operation takes on a

8.2. Complete scheme operations

single core. The total operations per second value quantifies the throughput, i.e., the amount of scheme operations, which are executed in one second on all scheme controllers in parallel.

For example, for the design variant 3SC3ST, 2000 scheme operations are executed on each scheme controller, which results in a total of 6000 operations distributed by the central core to the three scheme controllers in parallel. To get the core latency the overall execution time is divided by 2000. In contrast, the operations per second figure is computed as the reciprocal of the overall execution time divided by 6000.

The core latency and throughput values for complete scheme operations are shown in Tables 8.3 to 8.6. Each table contains the values for core latency and operations per second for the four operations *encryption*, *decryption*, *signing*, and *verification*, which were presented in Section 7.1. The tested bit-widths are those from Section 7.1.

Table 8.3.: Results for variant 4SC2ST

	Bit-width	Encryption Core latency	Encryption Total ops/sec	Decryption Core latency	Decryption Total ops/sec	Signing Core latency	Signing Total ops/sec	Verification Core latency	Verification Total ops/sec
RSA	1024	2.39 ms	1674.69	30.50 ms	131.16	30.36 ms	131.77	2.40 ms	1663.55
	1536	5.03 ms	795.47	97.53 ms	41.01	97.17 ms	41.17	5.01 ms	797.85
	2048	8.64 ms	462.83	225.03 ms	17.78	224.37 ms	17.83	8.59 ms	465.44
	3072	18.79 ms	212.87	741.23 ms	5.40	739.87 ms	5.41	18.68 ms	214.13
ECC	160	18.75 ms	213.28	9.59 ms	416.91	10.02 ms	399.34	18.78 ms	212.96
	192	29.47 ms	135.73	14.95 ms	267.50	15.74 ms	254.19	29.45 ms	135.84
	224	43.60 ms	91.74	21.94 ms	182.30	23.31 ms	171.61	43.60 ms	91.73
	256	61.85 ms	64.68	31.32 ms	127.72	33.08 ms	120.92	61.62 ms	64.91
PBC	512	–	–	–	–	266.51 ms	15.01	454.91 ms	8.79

Table 8.4.: Results for variant 3SC3ST

	Bit-width	Encryption Core latency	Encryption Total ops/sec	Decryption Core latency	Decryption Total ops/sec	Signing Core latency	Signing Total ops/sec	Verification Core latency	Verification Total ops/sec
RSA	1024	1.76 ms	1702.61	21.80 ms	137.64	21.64 ms	138.63	1.78 ms	1688.24
	1536	3.54 ms	847.70	66.91 ms	44.84	66.27 ms	45.27	3.52 ms	852.27
	2048	6.05 ms	495.99	157.31 ms	19.07	156.45 ms	19.18	6.00 ms	500.00
	3072	12.89 ms	232.72	499.26 ms	6.01	497.89 ms	6.03	12.78 ms	234.75
ECC	160	16.54 ms	181.37	8.46 ms	354.71	8.83 ms	339.92	16.26 ms	184.50
	192	22.51 ms	133.29	11.44 ms	262.35	12.00 ms	250.00	22.52 ms	133.22
	224	34.22 ms	87.66	17.36 ms	172.78	18.28 ms	164.13	34.12 ms	87.93
	256	49.70 ms	60.36	25.17 ms	119.20	26.57 ms	112.93	49.66 ms	60.41
PBC	512	–	–	–	–	188.94 ms	15.88	324.86 ms	9.23

A graphical representation of the throughput values is provided in Figures 8.1 to 8.4, which allow a better comparison between the same scheme operation on different design variants and between the same scheme operation from different public key approaches. Thus, the throughput values for the four operations encryption, decryption, signing, and verification are each shown in one of the graphs. The schemes are compared to each other based on the security level they provide in bits, see Section 7.1.

Table 8.5.: Results for variant 3SC4ST

	Bit-width	Encryption Core latency	Encryption Total ops/sec	Decryption Core latency	Decryption Total ops/sec	Signing Core latency	Signing Total ops/sec	Verification Core latency	Verification Total ops/sec
RSA	1024	1.39 ms	2162.16	16.68 ms	179.89	16.45 ms	182.33	1.40 ms	2142.86
	1536	2.80 ms	1072.96	51.54 ms	58.21	50.90 ms	58.94	2.78 ms	1080.11
	2048	4.69 ms	639.45	116.67 ms	25.71	115.81 ms	25.90	4.64 ms	646.41
	3072	9.94 ms	301.72	378.41 ms	7.93	377.05 ms	7.96	9.83 ms	305.13
ECC	160	14.32 ms	209.48	7.34 ms	408.47	7.64 ms	392.90	14.19 ms	211.37
	192	19.29 ms	155.49	9.83 ms	305.28	10.28 ms	291.96	19.19 ms	156.31
	224	29.85 ms	100.51	15.18 ms	197.61	15.93 ms	188.35	29.81 ms	100.63
	256	37.55 ms	79.89	18.99 ms	157.95	20.05 ms	149.65	37.41 ms	80.20
PBC	512	–	–	–	–	142.76 ms	21.01	247.46 ms	12.12

Table 8.6.: Results for variant 2SC6ST

	Bit-width	Encryption Core latency	Encryption Total ops/sec	Decryption Core latency	Decryption Total ops/sec	Signing Core latency	Signing Total ops/sec	Verification Core latency	Verification Total ops/sec
RSA	1024	1.08 ms	1857.01	13.33 ms	150.08	13.12 ms	152.40	1.09 ms	1831.50
	1536	2.05 ms	973.71	36.01 ms	55.54	35.68 ms	56.05	2.04 ms	981.11
	2048	3.46 ms	578.29	82.65 ms	24.20	82.17 ms	24.34	3.65 ms	548.70
	3072	7.00 ms	285.92	257.25 ms	7.77	256.52 ms	7.80	6.88 ms	290.59
ECC	192	16.62 ms	120.35	8.56 ms	233.63	8.84 ms	226.26	16.51 ms	121.12
	224	26.10 ms	76.64	13.32 ms	150.11	13.91 ms	143.75	25.88 ms	77.27
	256	32.53 ms	61.48	16.53 ms	120.97	17.37 ms	115.17	32.53 ms	61.48
PBC	512	–	–	–	–	113.22 ms	17.67	197.93 ms	10.10

Note that for both RSA and ECC the timing values of encryption and verification and the timing values for decryption and signing are similar. This is because of the similarity of the cryptographic main operations of these schemes. Both encryption and verification for RSA utilize the public key, which is set to $e = 2^{16} + 1$. The private key required for decryption and signing, in contrast, is an integer d with a large bit-width, thus, resulting in a much longer modular exponentiation. For ECC, in both encryption and verification two point multiplications are required each, while decryption and signing need just one point multiplication each.

Remember that for 2SC6ST no results are provided for ECC with a bit-width of 160, because the amount of 16 bit words must be at least the double of the number of pipeline stages, i.e., must be at least 12. Furthermore, for PBC only the BLS signature scheme was implemented, thus, results for PBC en-/decryption are omitted.

As can be seen from the graphs the design variant 3SC4ST is the most efficient for nearly all schemes. The only exception is ECC with 160 bit, where the fastest variant is 4SC2ST. This is somewhat surprising, as 3SC4ST contains a total of 24 pipeline stages[1], while 4SC2ST features only 16 pipeline stages. Thus, for this short bit-width added pipeline stages are not as beneficial as added parallel scheme executions.

Also interesting is the fact that while 3SC4ST, generally, is the best design variant, the second best variant is different for the respective public key approaches. For RSA

---

[1]Three ModArith cores containing each two modular multipliers with four stages each: $3 \cdot 2 \cdot 4 = 24$.

8.2. Complete scheme operations

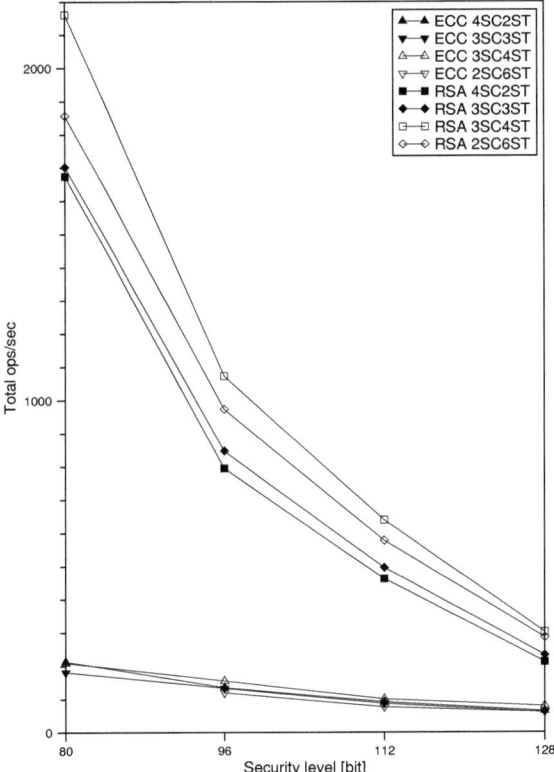

Figure 8.1.: Results for encryption schemes

and PBC with their rather long bit-widths the second-best variant is 2SC6ST. For ECC with its relatively short bit-widths the second-best variant is 4SC2ST.

This, however, is not really surprising. RSA and PBC require calculations on numbers with long bit-widths. Those benefit highly from the longer pipelines, as the overhead in this case is smaller: The difference between the required bit-widths and the actual computed bit-width[2] is relatively smaller and the longer pipelines utilize all stages in parallel for a longer amount of time[3]. In contrast, ECC features calculations with shorter bit-widths, which are not able to take advantage of the long pipelines to the same extent. Here, the higher parallelization of the scheme controllers in 4SC2ST contributes more to the efficiency.

---
[2] Remember that the pipelined multipliers always calculate a multiple of the number of stages in words.
[3] Remember that the pipelines have to be filled stage-by-stage before all stages are working concurrently.

Chapter 8. Results

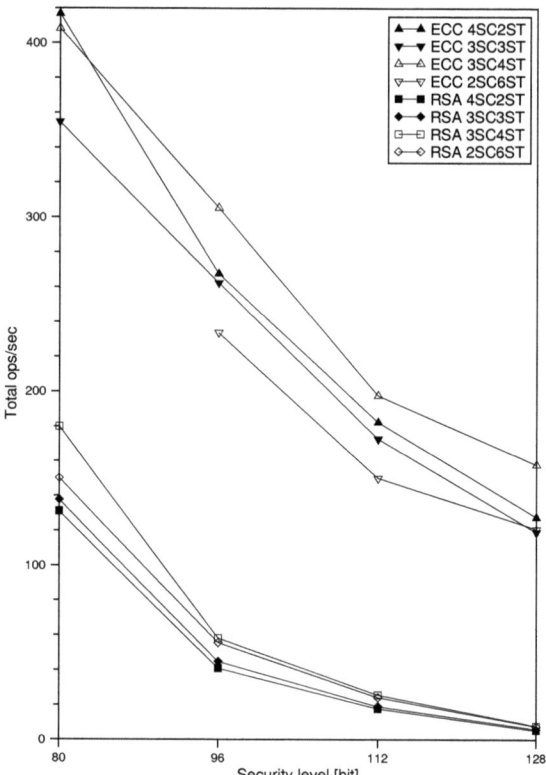

Figure 8.2.: Results for decryption schemes

Thus, as it was to be expected, the design variants with longer pipelines are better able to support calculations with larger bit-widths. The variants with shorter pipelines, at the same time, are better suited for computations with smaller bit-widths, as they parallelize the scheme execution to a higher degree. Further evidence for this relation can be found in the results. So does the efficiency of the variant 2SC6ST decrease less than that of 3SC3ST of ECC from 224 bit to 256 bit. Furthermore, while 4SC2ST is better than 3SC3ST for all ECC operations, it performs worse than 3SC3ST for all RSA and PBC operations.

This latter observation also leads to the conclusion that the important metric is not so much the lengths of the pipelines, but rather the total amount of pipeline stages. As 3SC3ST contains a total of 18 pipeline stages it should be faster than 4SC2ST, which contains only 16 pipeline stages. This advantage, however, asserts itself only for longer

8.2. Complete scheme operations

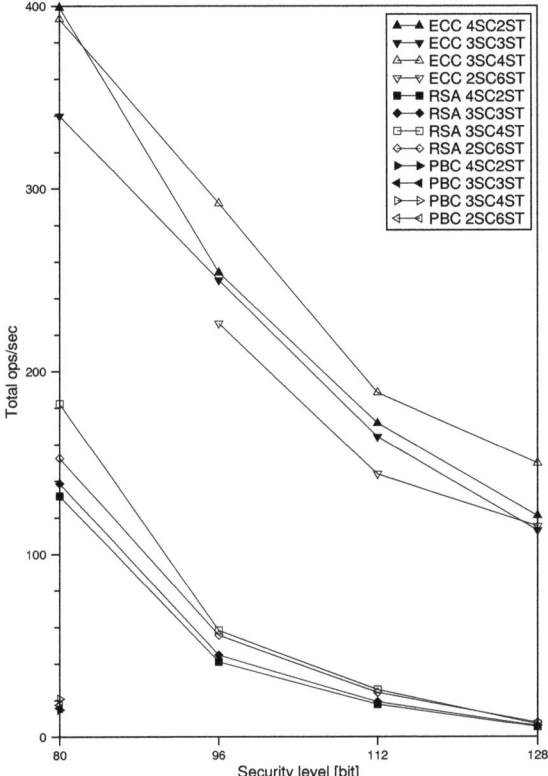

Figure 8.3.: Results for signing schemes

bit-widths. The variants 2SC6ST and 3SC4ST both contain a total of 24 pipeline stages. Therefore, the relation between them – i.e., 3SC4ST is more efficient – stays basically the same for all examined bit-widths.

Until now, it was not analyzed how the architecture scales with the number of scheme controllers. This is important, because both the central core and the AES core each exist just once. To examine this, all four design variants were tested with a different program for the PowerPC utilizing only the first MicroBlaze processor. The remaining soft-core processors were left unused.

The resulting timing values are depicted in Appendix B. Here, only the conclusions from these values are presented. From the experiments it can be derived that the sharing of both the central core and the AES core does, generally, not introduce any significant overhead. The difference between the latencies of the implementation exploiting all

Chapter 8. Results

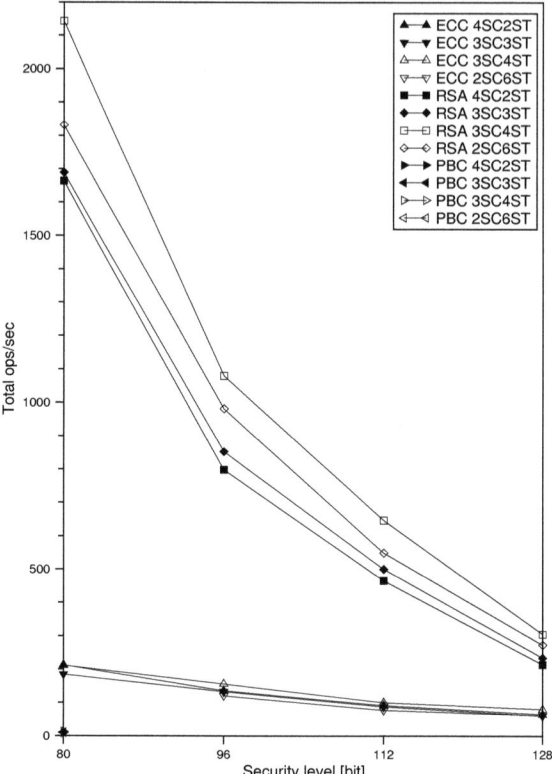

Figure 8.4.: Results for verification schemes

scheme controllers and that exploiting only the first controller is 0.00 ms or 0.01 ms in most cases, which is within the accuracy of measurement. There were, however, some exceptions:

1. The RSA decryption operation using all soft-cores exhibits a longer latency than that using just the first soft-core. Although the differences do not provide an uniform picture, they increase with the utilized bit-width.

2. The latency of the RSA signature verification on 2SC6ST with a bit-width of 2048 is 0.24 ms faster on the implementation exploiting only a single scheme controller.

3. The ECC operations – including the point multiplication – exhibit relatively high differences. In some cases the latency on the implementation using all scheme con-

trollers is even smaller than that on the implementation using just one controller. Furthermore, in contrast to RSA, the timing results are not deterministic, i.e., by repeating a test it was possible to get slightly different values. The differences in results were, usually, in the range of several 10 μs, but could increase up to several hundred μs. Therefore, by executing several test runs, results could be generated in many cases, which did not exhibit any difference between the implementations using all or just one scheme controller.

Unfortunately, there is no obvious reason for these differences, because the execution should be deterministic. Therefore, this area requires further study gaining insights in the inner workings leading to this slightly indeterministic behavior.

8.3. Cryptographic main operations

This section presents the timing values for just the cryptographic main operations of RSA and ECC without the execution of the other parts of the cryptographic schemes, i.e., mainly the auxiliary functions. These values are not that useful on their own, because a cryptographic main operation alone does not provide security. However, for realizations from literature, usually, only the results of the cryptographic main operations are provided. Thus, to ease the comparison with other designs in the next section, the cryptographic main operations were also measured alone. Additionally, this provides some clues to the execution time required for the auxiliary functions. Note that the timing values contain the time needed for the communication via the shared memory, because the scheme controllers are still operated by the central core.

Table 8.7.: Results of the cryptographic main operations for 4SC2ST and 3SC3ST

	Bit-width	4SC2ST		3SC3ST	
		Core latency	Total ops/sec	Core latency	Total ops/sec
Modular exponentiation (long exponent)	1024	30.08 ms	132.96	21.37 ms	140.39
	1536	96.78 ms	41.33	65.89 ms	45.53
	2048	223.88 ms	17.87	155.96 ms	19.24
	3072	739.15 ms	5.41	497.16 ms	6.03
Modular exponentiation (short exponent)	1024	2.11 ms	1894.84	1.48 ms	2020.88
	1536	4.62 ms	866.08	3.13 ms	959.23
	2048	8.07 ms	495.39	5.48 ms	547.70
	3072	17.94 ms	222.92	12.04 ms	249.11
Scalar multiplication	160	8.69 ms	460.22	7.66 ms	391.57
	192	13.68 ms	292.48	10.38 ms	288.88
	224	20.26 ms	197.46	15.90 ms	188.72
	256	28.73 ms	139.21	23.08 ms	129.98

Chapter 8. Results

Table 8.8.: Results of the cryptographic main operations for 3SC4ST and 2SC6ST

	Bit-width	3SC4ST Core latency	3SC4ST Total ops/sec	2SC6ST Core latency	2SC6ST Total ops/sec
Modular exponentiation (long exponent)	1024	16.18 ms	185.40	12.85 ms	155.61
	1536	50.52 ms	59.39	35.30 ms	56.66
	2048	115.32 ms	26.02	81.68 ms	24.49
	3072	376.33 ms	7.97	255.80 ms	7.82
Modular exponentiation (short exponent)	1024	1.11 ms	2696.63	803 μs	2493.77
	1536	2.38 ms	1257.86	1.64 ms	1216.55
	2048	4.12 ms	727.89	2.89 ms	691.92
	3072	9.10 ms	329.85	6.15 ms	325.07
Scalar multiplication	160	6.63 ms	452.52	–	–
	192	8.85 ms	338.93	7.66 ms	261.23
	224	13.86 ms	216.46	12.11 ms	165.19
	256	17.43 ms	172.16	15.10 ms	132.45

Table 8.7 shows the timing values for the variants 4SC2ST and 3SC3ST, while those for 3SC4ST and 2SC6ST are depicted in Table 8.8. The content of the table is similar to those in the previous section, although here the timings are for the modular exponentiation or the point multiplication. Because in RSA the modular exponentiation is exploited both with long/private and short/public exponent, the timings values for both types of exponentiation are provided.

A graphic representation of the timing results of the Cryptographic Main Operations can be found in Figures 8.5 and 8.6. They are structured similar to the graphs in the previous section. In this context, *ModExpLong* denotes a modular exponentiation with a long exponent, *ModExpLong* one with a short exponent, and *PointMult* stands for a scalar multiplication.

8.4. Comparison with other designs

Table 8.9 shows the performance figures of designs from literature. The second column contains the resource usage in terms of *logic cells* (LC) or *logic elements* (LE) for designs on Xilinx or Altera FPGAs, respectively. In this context, LC and LE are roughly comparable to each other, as both contain one LUT and one flipflop. Note that because the different references use different metrics to measure their resource usage, the conversion into LC/LE may not be exact in all cases.

The bit-width and the type of operation are given in the third and fourth column of Table 8.9, respectively. Unfortunately, only [38] provides values for complete scheme executions, while the remainder offers only the execution time for modular exponentiation and/or point multiplication. In this context, *Encryption* and *Decryption* denote the execution of a complete en-/decryption scheme. A modular exponentiation is named with

8.4. Comparison with other designs

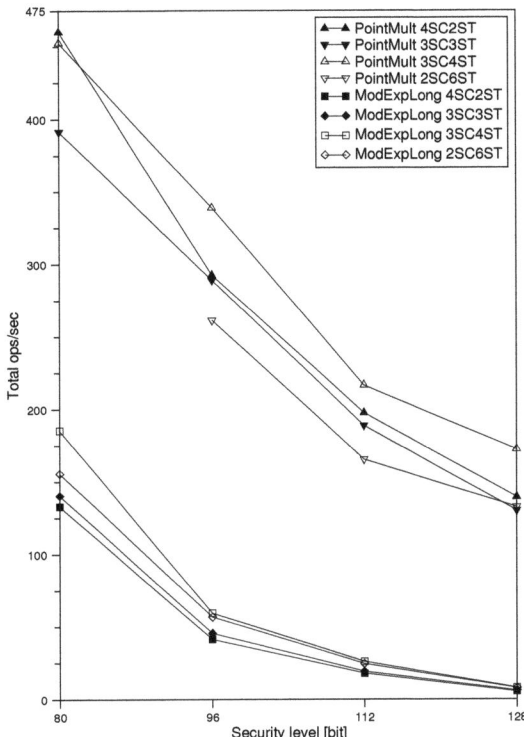

Figure 8.5.: Results for modular exponentiation with long exponent and point multiplication

ModExp (Encr) or *ModExp (Decr)*, where *Encr* indicates the usage of a short/public exponent and *Decr* that of a long/private exponent. *PointMult*, finally, stands for a point multiplication with a scalar of the given bit-width.

The remaining columns provide the latency and the throughput of the respective design. Values marked with '*' are estimated in this work, because the reference did provide just the execution time for a single modular multiplication.

Note that most references contain only the resources necessary to execute the respective cryptographic main operation, thus, their LC/LE should not be compared to the values from Table 8.1, but to those from Table 8.2. An exception are the single-chip designs from [38] and [25]. [38] includes cores for AES, SHA-1, RSA, and ECC over $\mathbb{GF}(2^m)$. [25] incorporates resources for AES, SHA-512, RSA, and memory control.

Compared to [38], all design variants from this work exhibit better performance. The

Chapter 8. Results

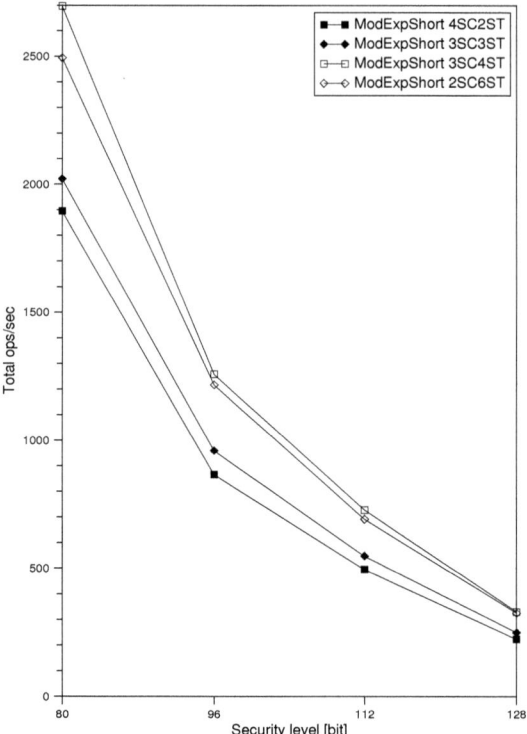

Figure 8.6.: Results for modular exponentiation with short exponent

higher throughput for the encryption in [38] stems most probably from the use of a shorter public exponent (only 5 bits) and from a different scheme for the encryption using other auxiliary functions. In comparison to [25], all design variants exhibit a better throughput, too, even in light of the fact that [25] does provide timing values for the modular exponentiations only.

Similar to this work, [26] tries to speed up RSA and ECC evenly on the same hardware. However, in [26] this is done by combining several multipliers for ECC into a larger one for RSA. Again, the design variants from this work exhibit better performance, perhaps because of the exploitation of the dedicated multipliers on the FPGA.

More optimized designs for ECC and RSA can be found in [72, 75]. Both have a considerable higher throughput than the variant 3SC4ST, see Table 8.8. However, remember that in 3SC4ST only 15876 LC are used for the modular arithmetic, while [72, 75] do not contain resources allowing the execution of complete schemes. Furthermore,

8.4. Comparison with other designs

both designs do not consider the calculation on numbers of other bit-widths, thus, are less flexible than the architecture from this work.

The realization from [117], which considers just RSA, employs two pipelined modular multipliers in parallel. Thus, it is somewhat similar to the design of the lowest level of the architecture proposed in this work. The values from [117] in Table 8.9 are from a variant with 16 pipeline stages in each multiplier. In comparison, the throughput of 3SC4ST is higher, even if the lower resource usage of [117] is taken into account.

[112] presents a pipelined modular multiplier able to operate on numbers of arbitrary bit-width. The values in Table 8.9 are from a variant with 16 pipeline stages exploiting the dedicated multipliers on a Virtex-II FPGA. If one takes into account the lower resource usage, it is faster than the prototype implementation. However, the design from [112] exploits both more dedicated multipliers and – more critically – more memory blocks, which were very scarce in the prototype implementation.

The design from [93] is a pure modular multiplication, too. It is realized as systolic array, which may be instantiated with different bit-widths. Table 8.9 provides the values for 256 and 1024 bit, respectively. For the given examples, both its size and timing values are worse than those from this work. However, it is to be expected that for variants with wider bit-widths the differences will get smaller, eventually reaching a point, where the design form [93] becomes faster than the prototype from this work. But then resources will stay unused for all multiplications on number with smaller bit-width, which will decrease throughput per used resource. The same considerations hold for the designs from [22, 21].

[8] presents a modular multiplier, which is able to operate on different bit-widths. Although it was not realized on an FPGA and, thus, the results are not directly comparable, it is included, because it was presented in Chapter 2 as related work.

The design from [14], finally, is considerably faster than the design from this work. However, like many other designs from literature, it only allows modular multiplication with a single bit-width. Thus, it does not allow the execution of complete schemes and is not able to operate on different bit-widths.

Unfortunately, a comparison of the PBC functionality of the design from this work is not possible, because literature on this topic seems to concentrate on implementations over $\mathbb{GF}(2^m)$, which can for example be found in [98, 110, 11].

Table 8.9.: Performance figures of comparable designs

Ref	LC/LE	Bit-width	Operation type	Latency	Ops/sec
[38]	28451 LE	1024	Encryption	0.25 ms	4000.00
			Decryption	31.93 ms	31.32
[25]	26880 LC	1024	ModExp (Decr)	20 ms	50.00
		2048	ModExp (Decr)	80 ms	12.50
[26]	10534 LC	256	PointMult	*26.50 ms	*39.06
		1033	ModExp (Decr)	*35.76 ms	*27.96
[72]	31510 LC	256	PointMult	3.86 ms	259.07
[75]	24324 LC	1024	ModExp (Decr)	3.829 ms	261.16
[117]	4112 LE	1024	ModExp (Encr)	7.8 ms	128.21
			ModExp (Decr)	39 ms	25.64
		2048	ModExp (Encr)	31 ms	32.26
			ModExp (Decr)	222 ms	4.50
[112]	4768 LC	1024	ModExp (Decr)	8.17 ms	122.40
[93]	3096 LC	256	PointMult	*35.41 ms	*28.24
	11412 LC	1024	ModExp (Decr)	*49.41 ms	*20.24
[22]	26604 LC	1024	ModExp (Decr)	27.25 ms	36.70
[21]	26836 LC	1024	ModExp (Decr)	27.36 ms	36.55
[8]	9094 gates	1024	ModExp (Decr)	15.2 ms	65.79
		1536	ModExp (Decr)	35 ms	28.57
		2048	ModExp (Decr)	60 ms	16.67
		4096	ModExp (Decr)	234ms	4.27
		139	PointMult	3.1 ms	322.58
		172	PointMult	4.7 ms	212.77
		197	PointMult	6.1 ms	163.93
		275	PointMult	6.7 ms	149.25
[14]	13266 LC	1024	ModExp (Encr)	0.22 ms	4545.45
	13652 LC	1024	ModExp (Decr)	3.10 ms	322.58

Chapter 9.
Conclusion

The architecture proposed in this work is able to support servers shouldering the load of secure communication with different client types using different cryptographic approaches. For this, the design exploits HW/SW co-design allowing the architecture to be both highly efficient and flexible concerning its supported schemes. The flexibility, which also allows relatively easy upgrades to new cryptographic schemes, aids long-term security, too, because it allows to substitute insecure schemes with secure ones.

The focus on the server-side shifts the performance goal into the direction of high throughput. This is in contrast to low latency, which is the usual metric in literature. However, these two goals do not always lead to the same designs, as the aim for flexibility and throughput limits the amount of parallelization and, thus, increases the latency. The low degree of parallelization on lower levels, however, can be compensated for by parallelization on higher levels.

These considerations led to the proposed flexible and efficient architecture for a cryptographic co-processor for server-application. Its performance figures are comparable to or better than those of designs from literature. Only highly optimized realizations with a comparable resource usage geared for a single bit-width outperform the presented prototype implementation. However, those do not offer the same flexibility and in their presented form are not yet able to execute complete schemes.

Although the prototype implementation illustrates the important points of the proposed architecture, it can not hide its proof-of-concept nature. For an usable version of the co-processor, the following improvements must/should be included, approximately in this order of importance.

- The complete functionality has to be executed on-chip to increase the security and the reusability. For this, firstly, additional memory is needed as instruction and data memory for the central core. Secondly, non-volatile memory is required for on-chip key storage, as, otherwise, the private keys would have to be loaded from the outside into the co-processor. Thirdly, the key generation for RSA must be possible on-chip, too. This may be done by exploiting the modular inversion according to the Extended Euclidean algorithm, which would have to be realized additionally. Note that this modular inversion may then also be used to speed up ECDSA.

- The communication with the host server should be realized using a faster bus, e.g.,

Ethernet. For this, of course, the program for the central core would have to be extended to actually receive commands from and send results to the host server.

- A further step to increase the usability of the implementation would be to allow the symmetric en-/decryption and hashing of larger amounts of data. As this does not concern data, which must be kept secret, off-chip memory may be used to store the initial and the encrypted data. The actual operation could be executed or controlled by the second PowerPC, which is left unused in the prototype implementation. Then, the host server may load the data to be encrypted/signed into the off-chip memory, from where the second PowerPC may read it. In case of encryption it writes the results back to this memory.

- A further improvement may be introduced by partly decoupling the communication between the central core and the scheme controllers allowing it to become asynchronous. If the size of the shared memory could be increased, the central core may store the data for several cryptographic scheme executions inside it. Then, the scheme controllers are able to operate more independently by looking whether a new command for an operation is waiting in the shared memory and execute it. This way, the respective parties do not have to wait for each other, which will increase the efficiency.

However, there are also some possible improvements to the proposed architecture, which were not considered in Chapter 6 for scope reasons.

- The modular arithmetic on the lowest level could be extended into a so called *unified architecture*, see [21, 31, 105], able to operate both in the finite fields $\mathbb{GF}(p)$ and $\mathbb{GF}(2^m)$. This is possible with a surprisingly small increase in resource usage, as the main difference is the propagation of the carry. Although those additional resources would not be useful for RSA, it would increase the flexibility of the architecture, which, then, would also be able to support ECC and PBC over $\mathbb{GF}(2^m)$. It is to be expected that those two approaches gain at least some acceptance, because they may be implemented in hardware with a considerable higher speed than those over $\mathbb{GF}(p)$.

- The modular multipliers in the ModArith core could also be extended according to the suggestion from [92, 91], allowing the computation of the elementary operations for the public key system NTRU, see [88]. Again, these additional resources could not be used for the other public key approaches. But the increase in flexibility may well be worth the expense.

- A different strategy for improvement would be the utilization of batch execution. This means that a *batch* of the same cryptographic operations with different keys and messages is calculated together allowing to exploit synergies between the single operations of the batch. For example, one could verify a batch of signatures together, which would then require only a fraction of the computational effort it would take to verify the signatures one-by-one. Possible approaches are proposed in [33, 5] for RSA and in [18, 81] for an identity-based scheme, i.e., for PBC. However, for the implementation of this, the amount of memory needs to be increased.

- A further improvement requiring additional memory is the exploitation of precomputation. For this, certain intermediate values of the cryptographic main operations are calculated beforehand and used to speed up the actual cryptographic main operation. This, however, is only useful, if the same precomputed values may be used for two or more cryptographic main operation. For example, one could precompute some multiples of the generator point of a curve, speeding up all computations on this curve. A possible approach is the idea from [65]. As mentioned above, however, this requires additional memory. Note that this may likely be combined with batch execution.

Appendix A.
Parameter set for Type A curves

The parameter set for the curve used in the prototype realization of PBC was taken from the PBC library, see [68]. In this work, only the so called *Type A Curves* were used, see [69] for details on the mathematical background. Below, the concrete parameter values for the curve used in the prototype are depicted. The prime q, the order of the curve n, the cofactor h, and the Weierstraß-coefficients a and b are part of the parameter set for the Type A curves. The coordinates of the generator point $G = (x_G, y_G)$ were generated using the PBC library.

$$\begin{aligned}
q &= \text{0xA7A73868E95FBA886EDEF8CE96E7217E364BB946F5ED839628D1F80010940622} \\
&\text{A7AFDAF9B049744A459E54DAB7BA5BE92539E8FF9B4F30A3CF6230C28E284D97} \\
h &= \text{0x14F4E70D1D2BF601BF6B0D47137CC83915F505F0E85050F93A6344777E2CD28F} \\
&\text{F9B4F30A3CF6230C28E284D98} \\
n &= \text{0x80000000000008000000000000000000000000001} \\
&= 2^{159} + 2^{107} + 1 \\
a &= \text{0x01} \\
b &= \text{0x00} \\
x_G &= \text{0x558639227C7254475195B4F6024AF058FDB2DD9F38F2A7DD2254642372196330} \\
&\text{C700B7E9B1087B7B3E4F9112711516080C22BD0ED29AC8E76880F764430BDA9A} \\
y_G &= \text{0x1B1D50976285DA33ADB0BA961B398AB7A39B0BA39FEC42184A37C616465CE47A} \\
&\text{861D442092D215A5885D61AF1E11902F96551FFB5F739C64520694007E4A2DC8}
\end{aligned}$$

Appendix B.
Timing values exploiting just one scheme controller

This chapter provides timing results similar to those in Chapter 8, but this time exploiting just one scheme controller. This means that the hardware of the designs was not changed. Only the program of the central core was modified in such a way that just the first scheme controller was issued the respective commands. This allows to compare the core latencies in the two cases that all or just one scheme controller is utilized. Thus, it can be observed how well the architecture scales with the number of scheme controllers, although it contains only one central core and only one AES core.

Note that the discussion on how well the architecture scales is part of Section 8.2. Here, only the concerned values are given. The timing results of complete scheme executions are provided in Tables B.1 to B.4. Table B.5 contains the timing values for the cryptographic main operations only. The structure of the tables is similar to that utilized in Chapter 8. However, the throughput values are omitted, because only the latency is of interest for considerations on the overhead.

Table B.1.: Latencies for 4SC2ST exploiting just one scheme controller

	Bit-width	Encryption	Decryption	Signing	Verification
RSA	1024	2.39 ms	30.39 ms	30.35 ms	2.40 ms
	1536	5.03 ms	97.23 ms	97.16 ms	5.01 ms
	2048	8.64 ms	224.45 ms	224.37 ms	8.59 ms
	3072	18.79 ms	740.04 ms	739.87 ms	18.67 ms
ECC	160	18.75 ms	9.52 ms	10.01 ms	18.56 ms
	192	29.46 ms	14.84 ms	15.73 ms	29.02 ms
	224	43.59 ms	22.01 ms	23.30 ms	43.50 ms
	256	61.84 ms	31.17 ms	33.06 ms	61.94 ms
PBC	512	—	—	266.50 ms	454.91 ms

Appendix B. Timing values exploiting just one scheme controller

Table B.2.: Latencies for 3SC3ST exploiting just one scheme controller

	Bit-width	Encryption	Decryption	Signing	Verification
RSA	1024	1.76 ms	21.68 ms	21.64 ms	1.78 ms
	1536	3.54 ms	66.34 ms	66.27 ms	3.52 ms
	2048	6.05 ms	156.57 ms	156.45 ms	6.00 ms
	3072	12.89 ms	498.07 ms	497.89 ms	12.78 ms
ECC	160	16.53 ms	8.40 ms	8.83 ms	16.35 ms
	192	22.50 ms	11.41 ms	12.00 ms	22.52 ms
	224	34.22 ms	17.23 ms	18.27 ms	34.13 ms
	256	49.68 ms	25.07 ms	26.53 ms	49.75 ms
PBC	512	–	–	188.94 ms	324.86 ms

Table B.3.: Latencies for 3SC4ST exploiting just one scheme controller

	Bit-width	Encryption	Decryption	Signing	Verification
RSA	1024	1.39 ms	16.49 ms	16.45 ms	1.40 ms
	1536	2.79 ms	50.97 ms	50.90 ms	2.78 ms
	2048	4.69 ms	115.93 ms	115.81 ms	4.64 ms
	3072	9.94 ms	377.23 ms	377.05 ms	9.83 ms
ECC	160	14.31 ms	7.29 ms	7.64 ms	14.15 ms
	192	19.29 ms	9.79 ms	10.28 ms	19.29 ms
	224	29.84 ms	15.04 ms	15.92 ms	29.76 ms
	256	37.53 ms	18.96 ms	20.02 ms	37.55 ms
PBC	512	–	–	142.76 ms	247.46 ms

Table B.4.: Latencies for 2SC6ST exploiting just one scheme controller

	Bit-width	Encryption	Decryption	Signing	Verification
RSA	1024	1.08 ms	13.16 ms	13.12 ms	1.09 ms
	1536	2.05 ms	35.76 ms	35.68 ms	2.04 ms
	2048	3.46 ms	82.28 ms	82.17 ms	3.41 ms
	3072	6.99 ms	256.71 ms	256.52 ms	6.88 ms
ECC	192	16.62 ms	8.45 ms	8.84 ms	16.55 ms
	224	26.09 ms	13.15 ms	13.91 ms	26.11 ms
	256	32.53 ms	16.45 ms	17.34 ms	32.35 ms
PBC	512	–	–	113.21 ms	197.92 ms

Table B.5.: Latencies for the cryptographic main operations exploiting just one scheme controller

	Bit-width	Latency			
		4SC2ST	3SC3ST	3SC4ST	2SC6ST
Modular exponentiation (long exponent)	1024	30.08 ms	21.37 ms	16.18 ms	12.85 ms
	1536	96.78 ms	65.89 ms	50.51 ms	35.30 ms
	2048	223.88 ms	155.96 ms	115.32 ms	81.68 ms
	3072	739.15 ms	497.17 ms	376.33 ms	255.80 ms
Modular exponentiation (short exponent)	1024	2.11 ms	1.49 ms	1.11 ms	802 μs
	1536	4.62 ms	3.13 ms	2.38 ms	1.64 ms
	2048	8.07 ms	5.48 ms	4.12 ms	2.89 ms
	3072	17.94 ms	12.04 ms	9.10 ms	6.15 ms
Scalar multiplication	160	8.48 ms	7.66 ms	6.63 ms	–
	192	13.68 ms	10.39 ms	8.90 ms	7.61 ms
	224	20.26 ms	15.75 ms	13.73 ms	12.11 ms
	256	28.74 ms	23.00 ms	17.36 ms	15.03 ms

Bibliography

[1] AOKI, K., HOSHINO, F., KOBAYASHI, T., AND OGURO, H. Elliptic Curve Arithmetic Using SIMD. In *International Conference on Information Security (ISC)* (2001), vol. 2200 of *Lecture Notes in Computer Science*, pp. 235–247.

[2] ARCTURUS NETWORKS INC. uCLinux – Embedded Linux/Microcontroller Project. http://www.uclinux.org/.

[3] AZIZ, A., AND IKRAM, N. An FPGA-based AES-CCM Crypto Core For IEEE 802.11i Architecture. *International Journal of Network Security 5*, 2 (2007), 224–232. http://ijns.nchu.edu.tw/contents/ijns-v5-n2/ijns-2007-v5-n2-p224-232.pdf.

[4] BAJARD, J., AND IMBERT, L. A Full RNS Implementation of RSA. *IEEE Trans. Computers 53*, 6 (2004), 769–774.

[5] BAO, F., LEE, C.-C., AND HWANG, M.-S. Cryptanalysis and improvement on batch verifying multiple RSA digital signatures. *Applied Mathematics and Computation 172*, 2 (2006), 1195–1200.

[6] BARKER, E., AND KELSEY, J. *NIST Special Publication 800-90 Recommendation for Random Number Generation Using Deterministic Random Bit Generators*, June 2006. http://csrc.nist.gov/publications/nistpubs/800-90/SP800-90_DRBG-June2006-final.pdf.

[7] BARRETT, P. Implementing the Rivest Shamir and Adleman Public Key Encryption Algorithm on a Standard Digital Signal Processor. In *Advances in Cryptology (CRYPTO)* (1986), vol. 263 of *Lecture Notes in Computer Science*, Springer, pp. 311–323.

[8] BATINA, L., BRUIN-MUURLING, G., AND ÖRS, S. B. Flexible Hardware Design for RSA and Elliptic Curve Cryptosystems. In *Topics in Cryptology - CT-RSA 2004* (2004), vol. 2964 of *Lecture Notes in Computer Science*, Springer, pp. 250–263.

[9] BEDNARA, M., DALDRUP, M., VON ZUR GATHEN, J., SHOKROLLAHI, J., AND TEICH, J. Reconfigurable Implementation of Elliptic Curve Crypto Algorithms. In *International Parallel and Distributed Processing Symposium (IPDPS)* (2002). http://www-math.upb.de/~aggathen/Publications/raw02.pdf.

[10] BERTONI, G., BREVEGLIERI, L., WOLLINGER, T. J., AND PAAR, C. Finding Optimum Parallel Coprocessor Design for Genus 2 Hyperelliptic Curve Cryptosystems. In *International Conference on Information Technology: Coding and Computing (ITCC)* (2004), vol. 2, pp. 538–544. http://citeseer.ist.psu.edu/bertoni04finding.html.

[11] BEUCHAT, J.-L., BRISEBARRE, N., DETREY, J., AND OKAMOTO, E. Arithmetic Operators for Pairing-Based Cryptography. In *Workshop on Cryptographic Hardware and Embedded Systems (CHES)* (2007), vol. 4727 of *Lecture Notes in Computer Science*, pp. 239–255.

[12] BLAKE, I. F., SEROUSSI, G., AND SMART, N. P. *Elliptic Curves in Cryptography*. Cambridge University Press, New York, NY, USA, 1999.

[13] BLAKE, I. F., SEROUSSI, G., AND SMART, N. P., Eds. *Advances in Elliptic Curve Cryptography*. Cambridge University Press, New York, NY, USA, 2005.

[14] BLUM, T., AND PAAR, C. High-Radix Montgomery Modular Exponentiation on Reconfigurable Hardware. *IEEE Trans. Comput. 50*, 7 (2001), 759–764.

[15] BLÜMEL, R., LAUE, R., AND HUSS, S. A. A highly efficient modular Multiplication Algorithm for Finite Field Arithmetic in $\mathbb{GF}(P)$. In *ECRYPT Workshop: CRyptographic Advances in Secure Hardware (CRASH)* (Sept. 2005). http://www.vlsi.informatik.tu-darmstadt.de/staff/laue/publications/crash2005.html.

[16] BONEH, D., LYNN, B., AND SHACHAM, H. Short Signatures from the Weil Pairing. In *ASIACRYPT '01: Proceedings of the 7th International Conference on the Theory and Application of Cryptology and Information Security* (2001), Springer-Verlag, pp. 514–532.

[17] BRAUN, N., AND SIKORA, A. Design Strategies for Secure Embedded Networking. In *Workshop 'Long-term Security', Emerging Trends in Information and Communication Security (ETRICS)* (Freiburg, Germany, June 2006).

[18] CHEON, J. H., KIM, Y., AND YOON, H. J. A New ID-based Signature with Batch Verification. Cryptology ePrint Archive, Report 2004/131, 2004. http://eprint.iacr.org/2004/131.

[19] CHODOWIEC, P., AND GAJ, K. Very Compact FPGA Implementation of the AES Algorithm. In *Workshop on Cryptographic Hardware and Embedded Systems (CHES)* (2003), vol. 2779 of *Lecture Notes in Computer Science*, Springer, pp. 319–333.

[20] CIET, M., NEVE, M., PEETERS, E., AND QUISQUATER, J.-J. Parallel FPGA Implementation of RSA with Residue Number Systems - Can side-channel threats be avoided? In *IEEE Midwest International Symposium on Circuits and Systems* (2003). http://eprint.iacr.org/2004/187.

Bibliography

[21] CILARDO, A., MAZZEO, A., MAZZOCCA, N., AND ROMANO, L. A Novel Unified Architecture for Public-Key Cryptography. In *Conference on Design, Automation and Test in Europe (DATE)* (Washington, DC, USA, 2005), IEEE Computer Society, pp. 52–57.

[22] CILARDO, A., MAZZEO, A., ROMANO, L., AND SAGGESE, G. P. Carry-Save Montgomery Modular Exponentiation on Reconfigurable Hardware. In *Design, Automation and Test in Europe (DATE)* (2004), IEEE Computer Society, pp. 206–211.

[23] COHEN, B., AND LAURIE, B. AES-hash, May 2001. http://csrc.nist.gov/encryption/modes/proposedmodes/aes-hash/aeshash.pdf.

[24] COHEN, H., MIYAJI, A., AND ONO, T. Efficient Elliptic Curve Exponentiation Using Mixed Coordinates. In *ASIACRYPT '98: Proceedings of the International Conference on the Theory and Applications of Cryptology and Information Security* (London, UK, 1998), Springer-Verlag, pp. 51–65.

[25] CROWE, F., DALY, A., KERINS, T., AND MARNANE, W. P. Single-Chip FPGA Implementation of a Cryptographic Co-Processor. In *International Conference on Field-Programmable Technology (FPT)* (Dec. 2004), pp. 279–285.

[26] CROWE, F., DALY, A., AND MARNANE, W. P. A Scalable Dual Mode Arithmetic Unit for Public Key Cryptosystems. In *International Conference on Information Technology: Coding and Computing (ITCC)* (2005), vol. 1, IEEE Computer Society, pp. 568–573.

[27] DAEMEN, J., AND RIJMEN, V. *The Design of Rijndael*. Springer, Secaucus, NJ, USA, 2002.

[28] DE MACEDO MOURELLE, L., AND NEDJAH, N. Efficient Cryptographic Hardware Using the Co-Design Methodology. In *International Conference on Information Technology: Coding and Computing (ITCC)* (Washington, DC, USA, 2004), vol. 2, IEEE Computer Society, pp. 508–512.

[29] DHEM, J.-F., AND QUISQUATER, J.-J. Recent Results on Modular Multiplications for Smart Cards. In *International Conference on Smart Card Research and Applications (CARDIS)* (London, UK, 2000), Springer-Verlag, pp. 336–352.

[30] DUTTA, R., BARUA, R., AND SARKAR, P. Pairing-Based Cryptographic Protocols: A Survey. Tech. Rep. 2004/064, IACR eprint archive, 2004. http://eprint.iacr.org/2004/064.

[31] EBERLE, H., GURA, N., SHANTZ, S. C., GUPTA, V., RARICK, L., AND SUNDARAM, S. A Public-Key Cryptographic Processor for RSA and ECC. In *International Conference on Application-Specific Systems, Architectures and Processors (ASAP)* (Washington, DC, USA, 2004), IEEE Computer Society, pp. 98–110.

[32] ECRYPT NETWORK OF EXCELLENCE. *Side Channel Cryptanalysis Lounge.* http://www.crypto.ruhr-uni-bochum.de/en_sclounge.html.

[33] FIAT, A. Batch RSA. *Journal of Cryptology 10*, 2 (1997), 75–88.

[34] FISCHER, W., GIRAUD, C., AND KNUDSEN, E. W. Parallel scalar multiplication on general elliptic curves over $\mathbb{F}_p$ hedged against Non-Differential Side-Channel Attacks. Tech. Rep. 2002/007, IACR eprint archive, Jan. 2002. http://eprint.iacr.org/2002/007.pdf.

[35] GOOD, T., AND BENAISSA, M. AES on FPGA from the Fastest to the Smallest. In *Workshop on Cryptographic Hardware and Embedded Systems (CHES)* (2005), vol. 3659 of *Lecture Notes in Computer Science*, Springer, pp. 427–440.

[36] GORDON, D. M. A survey of fast exponentiation methods. *Journal of Algorithms 27*, 1 (1998), 129–146.

[37] GUPTA, V., STEBILA, D., FUNG, S., SHANTZ, S. C., GURA, N., AND EBERLE, H. Speeding up Secure Web Transactions Using Elliptic Curve Cryptography. In *Proceedings of the Network and Distributed System Security Symposium (NDSS)* (San Diego, California, USA, 2004), The Internet Society.

[38] HANI, M. K., WEN, H. Y., AND PANIANDI, A. Design and Implementation of a Private and Public Key Crypto Processor for Next-Generation IT Security Applications. *Malaysian Journal of Computer Science 19*, 1 (2006).

[39] HANKERSON, D., MENEZES, A. J., AND VANSTONE, S. *Guide to Elliptic Curve Cryptography.* Springer-Verlag New York, Secaucus, NJ, USA, 2003.

[40] HELION TECHNOLOGY. *DATASHEET - Tiny Multi-mode Hash Core for Xilinx FPGA*, 2005. http://www.heliontech.com/multihash.htm.

[41] HUNGERFORD, T. W. *Algebra.* Graduate Texts in Mathematics. Springer-Verlag, 1974.

[42] IEEE. *IEEE 1363-2000: Standard Specifications for Public-Key Cryptography.* New York, USA, 2000. http://grouper.ieee.org/groups/1363/.

[43] IEEE. *IEEE 1363a-2004: Standard Specifications for Public-Key Cryptography – Amendment 1: Additional Techniques.* New York, USA, 2004. http://grouper.ieee.org/groups/1363/.

[44] INSTITUTE FOR COMPUTER ALGEBRA, DISTRIBUTED SYSTEMS AND CRYPTOGRAPHY (CDC), COMPUTER SCIENCE DEPARTMENT, TECHNISCHE UNIVERSITÄT DARMSTADT. LiDIA - A C++ Library For Computational Number Theory. http://www.cdc.informatik.tu-darmstadt.de/TI/LiDIA/.

[45] IZU, T., AND TAKAGI, T. A Fast Parallel Elliptic Curve Multiplication Resistant against Side Channel Attacks. In *International Workshop on Practice and Theory in Public Key Cryptosystems: Public Key Cryptography* (2002), vol. 2274 of *Lecture Notes in Computer Science*, pp. 280–296.

[46] IZU, T., AND TAKAGI, T. Efficient Computations of the Tate Pairing for the Large MOV Degrees. In *International Conference Information Security and Cryptology (ICISC)* (2002), vol. 2587 of *Lecture Notes in Computer Science*, Springer, pp. 283–297.

[47] IZU, T., AND TAKAGI, T. Fast Elliptic Curve Multiplications with SIMD Operations. In *International Conference on Information and Communications Security (ICICS)* (2002), vol. 2513 of *Lecture Notes in Computer Science*, pp. 217–230. http://www.fun.ac.jp/~takagi/takagi/publications/icics02_simd.pdf.

[48] JANSSENS, S., THOMAS, J., BORREMANS, W., GIJSELS, P., VERHAUWHEDE, I., VERCAUTEREN, F., PRENEEL, B., AND VANDEWALLE, J. Hardware/software Co-Design Of An Elliptic Curve Public-Key Cryptosystem. In *IEEE Workshop on of Signal Processing Systems* (2001), pp. 209–216. http://citeseer.ist.psu.edu/janssens01hardwaresoftware.html.

[49] JHUMKA, A., KLAUS, S., AND HUSS, S. A. A Dependability-Driven System-Level Design Approach for Embedded Systems. In *Design, Automation and Test in Europe (DATE)* (2005), IEEE Computer Society, pp. 372–377.

[50] JOYE, M., AND YEN, S.-M. The Montgomery Powering Ladder. In *Workshop on Cryptographic Hardware and Embedded Systems (CHES)* (2002), vol. 2523 of *Lecture Notes in Computer Science*, pp. 291–302. http://www.gemplus.com/smart/rd/publications/pdf/JY03mont.pdf.

[51] KELLEY, K., AND HARRIS, D. Parallelized Very High Radix Scalable Montgomery Multipliers. In *Thirty-Ninth Asilomar Conference on Signals, Systems and Computers* (2005), pp. 1196–1200.

[52] KELLEY, K., AND HARRIS, D. Very High Radix Scalable Montgomery Multipliers. In *International Workshop on System-on-Chip for Real-Time Applications (IWSOC)* (Washington, DC, USA, 2005), IEEE Computer Society, pp. 400–404.

[53] KENT, S., AND ATKINSON, R. Security Architecture for the Internet Protocol. Tech. Rep. RCF 2401, IETF, Nov. 1998. http://tools.ietf.org/html/rfc2401.

[54] KLAUS, S. *System-Level-Entwurfsmethodik eingebetteter Systeme*. PhD thesis, Technische Universität Darmstadt, 2005. (in German).

[55] KLAUS, S., AND HUSS, S. A. Konzepte zur Beherrschung der Entwurfskomplexität eingebetteter Systeme. *it - Information Technology, Methoden und innovative Anwendungen der Informatik und Informationstechnik 46*, 2 (2004), 59–66. (in German).

[56] KOBLITZ, N. Elliptic Curve Cryptosystems. *Mathematics of Computation 48*, 177 (Jan. 1987), 203–209.

[57] KÜHN, U. Aktuelle Entwicklungen bei RSA-Signaturen. *Datenschutz und Datensicherheit 30*, 12 (2006), 763–767. (in German).

[58] LAUE, R., AND HUSS, S. A. A Novel Memory Architecture for Elliptic Curve Cryptography with Parallel Modular Multipliers. In *IEEE International Conference on Field Programmable Technology (FPT)* (Bangkok, Thailand, 2006), IEEE Computer Society, pp. 149–156.

[59] LAUE, R., AND HUSS, S. A. Perfomanter Krypto-CoProzessor für unterschiedliche Verfahren. In *5. Krypto-Tag - Workshop über Kryptographie*, H. Stamer, Ed., no. 06 in Mathematische Schriften Kassel. Universität Kassel, 2006, p. 3. (in German).

[60] LAUE, R., AND HUSS, S. A. Parallel Memory Architecture for Elliptic Curve Cryptography over $\mathbb{GF}(p)$ Aimed at Efficient FPGA Implementation. *Journal of Signal Processing Systems 51*, 1 (2008), 39–55.

[61] LAUE, R., KELM, O., SCHIPP, S., SHOUFAN, A., AND HUSS, S. A. Compact AES-based Architecture for Symmetric Encryption, Hash Function, and Random Number Generation. In *International Conference on Field Programmable Logic and Applications (FPL)* (Amsterdam, Netherlands, 2007), pp. 480–484.

[62] LAUE, R., MOLTER, H. G., RIEDER, F., SAXENA, K., AND HUSS, S. A. A Novel Multiple Core Co-Processor Architecture for Efficient Server-based Public Key Cryptography Applications. In *IEEE Computer Society Anuual Symposium an VLSI (ISVLSI)* (Montpellier, France, Apr. 2008), pp. 149–156.

[63] LENSTRA, A. K., AND VERHEUL, E. R. Selecting Cryptographic Key Sizes. *Journal of Cryptology 14*, 4 (2001), 255–293.

[64] LEUNG, K. H., MA, K. W., WONG, W. K., AND LEONG, P. H. W. FPGA Implementation of a Microcoded Elliptic Curve Cryptographic Processor. In *Symposium on Field-Programmable Custom Computing Machines (FCCM)* (Washington, DC, USA, 2000), IEEE Computer Society, pp. 68–76.

[65] LIM, C. H., AND LEE, P. J. More Flexible Exponentiation with Precomputation. In *CRYPTO '94: Proceedings of the 14th Annual International Cryptology Conference on Advances in Cryptology* (1994), Y. G. Desmedt, Ed., vol. 839 of *Lecture Notes in Computer Science*, pp. 95–107. citeseer.ist.psu.edu/lim94more.html.

[66] LIPMAA, H., ROGAWAY, P., AND WAGNER, D. Comments to NIST Concerning AES Modes of Operations: CTR-Mode Encryption. In *Symmetric Key Block Cipher Modes of Operation Workshop* (Baltimore, Maryland, USA, 2000). http://citeseer.ist.psu.edu/lipmaa00comments.html.

[67] LU, J., AND LOCKWOOD, J. IPSec Implementation on Xilinx Virtex-II Pro FPGA and Its Application. In *Proceedings of the 19th IEEE International Parallel and Distributed Processing Symposium (IPDPS) - Workshop 3* (Washington, DC, USA, 2005), IEEE Computer Society, p. 158.2.

[68] LYNN, B. The pairing-based cryptography library. http://crypto.stanford.edu/pbc/.

[69] LYNN, B. *On the Implementation of Pairing-Based Cryptosystems.* PhD thesis, Stanford University, June 2007.

[70] MARCUS STÖGBAUER. *Efficient Algorithms for Pairing-Based Cryptosystems.* Technische Universität Darmstadt, Darmstadt, 2004. Diplom Thesis, http://www.cdc.informatik.tu-darmstadt.de/reports/reports/Marcus_Stoegbauer.diplom.pdf.

[71] MATYAS, S., MEYER, C., AND OSEAS, J. Generating Strong One-Way Functions with Cryptographic Algorithm. *IBM Technical Disclosure Bulletin 27*, 10A (Mar. 1985), 5658–5659.

[72] MCIVOR, C. J., MCLOONE, M., AND MCCANNY, J. V. Hardware Elliptic Curve Cryptographic Processor Over $\mathbb{GF}(p)$. *IEEE Transactions on Circuits and Systems I: Regular Papers 53*, 9 (2006), 1946–1957.

[73] MCLOONE, M., AND MCCANNY, J. V. A single-chip IPSEC cryptographic processor. In *IEEE Workshop on Signal Processing Systems (SIPS)* (2002), pp. 133–138.

[74] MENEZES, A. J., VAN OORSCHOT, P. C., AND VANSTONE, S. A. *Handbook of Applied Cryptography.* CRC Press series on discrete mathematics and its applications. CRC Press, 1997. http://www.cacr.math.uwaterloo.ca/hac/.

[75] MICHALSKI, A., AND BUELL, D. A Scalable Architecture for RSA Cryptography on Large FPGAs. In *IEEE Symposium on Field-Programmable Custom Computing Machines (FCCM)* (2006), IEEE Computer Society, pp. 331–332.

[76] MILLER, V. Short program for functions on curves. Unpublished manuscript, urlhttp://citeseer.ist.psu.edu/miller86short.html, 1986.

[77] MILLER, V. S. Use of Elliptic Curves in Cryptography. In *Advances in Cryptology (CRYPTO)* (Aug. 1985), H. C. Williams, Ed., vol. 218 of *Lecture Notes in Computer Science*, Springer-Verlag, 1986, pp. 417–426.

[78] MISHRA, P. K. Pipelined Computation of Scalar Multiplication in Elliptic Curve Cryptosystems. In *Workshop on Cryptographic Hardware and Embedded Systems (CHES)* (2004), vol. 3156 of *Lecture Notes in Computer Science*, pp. 328–342.

[79] MOLTER, G. *Flexibler Krypto-CoProzessor für Server als SoC*. Technische Universität Darmstadt, Darmstadt, 2007. Diplom Thesis (in German), http://www.vlsi.informatik.tu-darmstadt.de/staff/laue/arbeiten/molter_thesis.pdf.

[80] MONTGOMERY, P. L. Modular Multiplication Without Trial Division. *Mathematics of Computation 44*, 170 (Apr. 1985), 519–521.

[81] NAD JUNG HEE CHEON, H. J. Y., AND KIM, Y. Batch Verifications with ID-Based Signatures. In *Information Security and Cryptology (ICISC)* (2005), vol. 3506 of *Lecture Notes in Computer Science*, pp. 233–248.

[82] NAKAMULA, K. A Survey on the Number Field Sieve. In *Number Theory and Its Applications*, S. Kanemitsu and K. Gyory, Eds., vol. 2 of *Developments in Mathematics*. Springer, 1999.

[83] NATIONAL INSTITUTE OF STANDARDS AND TECHNOLOGY. FIPS PUB 197: Advanced Encryption Standard (AES), Nov. 2001. http://csrc.nist.gov/publications/PubsFIPS.html.

[84] NATIONAL INSTITUTE OF STANDARDS AND TECHNOLOGY. FIPS PUB 198: The Keyed-Hash Message Authentication Code (HMAC), Mar. 2002. http://csrc.nist.gov/publications/PubsFIPS.html.

[85] NATIONAL INSTITUTE OF STANDARDS AND TECHNOLOGY. FIPS PUB 186-3: Digital Signature Standard (DSS), Mar. 2006. http://csrc.nist.gov/publications/PubsFIPS.html.

[86] NEDJAH, N., AND DE MACEDO MOURELLE, L. Reconfigurable Hardware Implementation of Montgomery Modular Multiplication and Parallel Binary Exponentiation. In *Euromicro Symposium on Digital Systems Design (DSD)* (2002), IEEE Computer Society, pp. 226–235.

[87] NEDJAH, N., AND DE MACEDO MOURELLE, L. Fast Less Recursive Hardware for Large Number Multiplication Using Karatsuba-Ofman's Algorithm. In *International Symposium on Computer and Information Sciences (ISCIS)* (2003), vol. 2869 of *Lecture Notes in Computer Science*, pp. 43–50.

[88] NTRU CRYPTOSYSTEMS, INC. *NTRU CryptoLab*. http://www.ntru.com/cryptolab/index.htm.

[89] OHBA, N., AND TAKANO, K. An SoC design methodology using FPGAs and embedded microprocessors. In *Conference on Design automation (DAC)* (New York, NY, USA, 2004), ACM Press, pp. 747–752.

[90] ORLANDO, G., AND PAAR, C. A Scalable $\mathbb{GF}(p)$ Elliptic Curve Processor Architecture for Programmable Hardware. In *Workshop on Cryptographic Hardware*

and *Embedded Systems (CHES)* (2001), vol. 2162 of *Lecture Notes in Computer Science*, pp. 348–363. http://www.crypto.ruhr-uni-bochum.de/imperia/md/content/texte/ecpp_ches.pdf.

[91] O'ROURKE, C., AND SUNAR, B. Achieving NTRU with Montgomery Multiplication. *IEEE Trans. Computers 52*, 4 (2003), 440–448.

[92] O'ROURKE, C. M. Efficient NTRU Implementations. Master's thesis, Worcester Polytechnic Institute, Apr. 2002.

[93] ÖRS, S. B., BATINA, L., PRENEEL, B., AND VANDEWALLE, J. Hardware Implementation of a Montgomery Modular Multiplier in a Systolic Array. In *International Parallel and Distributed Processing Symposium (IPDPS)* (2003), IEEE Computer Society, p. 184. http://www.cosic.esat.kuleuven.be/publications/article-32.pdf.

[94] PLATTE, J., AND NAROSKA, E. A Combined Hardware and Software Architecture for Secure Computing. In *Conference on Computing Frontiers (CF)* (New York, NY, USA, 2005), ACM Press, pp. 280–288.

[95] RIEDER, F. *Modular Multiplikation mit kurzen Pipelines*. Technische Universität Darmstadt, Darmstadt, 2008. Diplom Thesis (in German), http://www.vlsi.informatik.tu-darmstadt.de/staff/laue/arbeiten/rieder_thesis.pdf.

[96] RIVEST, R., SHAMIR, A., AND ADLEMAN, L. A Method for Obtaining Digital Signatures and Public Key Cryptosystems. *Communications of the ACM 21*, 2 (Feb. 1978), 120–126.

[97] RODRÍGUEZ-HENRÍQUEZ, F., AND ÇETIN KAYA KOÇ. On fully parallel Karatsuba Multipliers for $GF(2^m)$. In *International Conference on Computer Science and Technology (CST)* (Cancún, México, May 2003), Acta Press, pp. 405–410. http://security.ece.orst.edu/papers/c29fpkar.pdf.

[98] RONAN, R., O'HEIGEARTAIGH, C., MURPHY, C., SCOTT, M., AND KERINS, T. FPGA Acceleration of the Tate Pairing in Characteristic 2. In *IEEE International Conference on Field Programmable Technology (FPT)* (Bangkok, Thailand, 2006), IEEE Computer Society, pp. 149–156.

[99] ROUVROY, G., STANDAERT, F.-X., QUISQUATER, J.-J., AND LEGAT, J.-D. Compact and Efficient Encryption/Decryption Module for FPGA Implementation of AES Rijndael Very Well Suited for Small Embedded Apllications. In *International Conference on Information Technology: Coding and Computing (ITCC)* (2004), vol. 2, IEEE Computer Society, pp. 583–587.

[100] RSA LABORATORIES. *PKCS #1 v2.1: RSA Cryptography Standard*, June 2002. ftp://ftp.rsasecurity.com/pub/pkcs/pkcs-1/pkcs-1v2-1.pdf.

[101] SAKIYAMA, K., BATINA, L., PRENEEL, B., AND VERBAUWHEDE, I. HW/SW Co-design for Accelerating Public-Key Cryptosystems over GF(p) on the 8051 μ-controller. In *Proceedings of World Automation Congress (WAC)* (2006).

[102] SAKIYAMA, K., BATINA, L., PRENEEL, B., AND VERBAUWHEDE, I. Superscalar Coprocessor for High-Speed Curve-Based Cryptography. In *Workshop on Cryptographic Hardware and Embedded Systems (CHES)* (2006), vol. 4249 of *Lecture Notes in Computer Science*, Springer, pp. 415–429.

[103] SANU, M. O., JR., E. E. S., AND CHASE, C. M. Parallel Montgomery Multipliers. In *International Conference on Application-Specific Systems, Architectures, and Processors (ASAP)* (2004), IEEE Computer Society, pp. 63–72.

[104] SAQIB, N. A., RODRÍGUEZ-HENRÍQUEZ, F., AND DÍAZ-PÉREZ, A. A Parallel Architecture for Computing Scalar Multiplication on Hessian Elliptic Curves. In *International Conference on Information Technology: Coding and Computing (ITCC)* (2004), vol. 2, pp. 493–497.

[105] SATOH, A., AND TAKANO, K. A Scalable Dual-Field Elliptic Curve Cryptographic Processor. *IEEE Trans. Comput. 52*, 4 (2003), 449–460.

[106] SAWYER, N., AND DEFOSSEZ, M. *Quad-Port Memories in Virtex Devices*. XILINX, Sept. 2002. http://direct.xilinx.com/bvdocs/appnotes/xapp228.pdf.

[107] SCHINIANAKIS, D., FOURNARIS, A., KAKAROUNTAS, A. P., AND STOURAITIS, T. An RNS Architecture of an $\mathbb{F}_p$ Elliptic Curve Point Multiplier. In *IEEE International Symposium on Circuits and Systems (ISCAS)* (2006), pp. 3369–3373.

[108] SCHNEIER, B. *Applied Cryptography: Protocols, Algorithms, and Source Code in C*, 2nd ed. Wiley, New York, 1996.

[109] SCOTT, M. *Deterministic Hashing to points on IBE-friendly elliptic curves*. School of Computing, Dublin City University, May 2005. ftp://ftp.computing.dcu.ie/pub/resources/crypto/cth.pdf.

[110] SHU, C., KWON, S., AND GAJ, K. FPGA Accelerated Tate Pairing Based Cryptosystems over Binary Fields. In *IEEE International Conference on Field Programmable Technology (FPT)* (Bangkok, Thailand, 2006), IEEE Computer Society, pp. 149–156. http://citeseer.ist.psu.edu/759907.html.

[111] SMITH, M. J. S. *Application-Specific Integrated Circuits*. Addison-Wesley Longman Publishing Co., Inc., Boston, MA, USA, 1997.

[112] TAMER GÜDÜ. A new Scalable Hardware Architecture for RSA Algorithm. In *International Conference on Field Programmable Logic and Applications (FPL)* (Amsterdam, Netherlands, 2007), pp. 670–674.

[113] TENCA, A. F., AND Ç. K. KOÇ. A Scalable Architecture for Montgomery Multiplication. In *Workshop on Cryptographic Hardware and Embedded Systems (CHES)* (London, UK, 1999), vol. 1717 of *Lecture Notes in Computer Science*, Springer-Verlag, pp. 94–108. http://www.security.ece.orst.edu/koc/papers/c17.pdf.

[114] TENCA, A. F., AND Ç. K. KOÇ. A Scalable Architecture for Modular Multiplication Based on Montgomery's Algorithm. *IEEE Trans. Computers 52*, 9 (2003), 1215–1221. http://www.comelec.enst.fr/enseignement/briques/aaa/publis/crypto/rsa_scalable.pdf.

[115] TSOI, K. H., LEUNG, K. H., AND LEONG, P. H. W. Compact FPGA-based True and Pseudo Random Number Generators. In *Symposium on Field-Programmable Custom Computing Machines (FCCM)* (Washington, DC, USA, 2003), IEEE Computer Society, pp. 51–61.

[116] VANSTONE, S. A. Next generation security for wireless: elliptic curve cryptography. *Computers & Security 22*, 5 (2003), 412–415.

[117] ŠIMKA, M., FISCHER, V., AND DRUTAROVSKÝ, M. Hardware-Software Codesign in Embedded Asymmetric Cryptography Application – a Case Study. In *Field-Programmable Logic and Applications (FPL)* (Lisbon, Portugal, Sept. 2003), vol. 2778 of *Lecture Notes in Computer Science*, pp. 1075–1078. http://citeseer.ist.psu.edu/simka03hardwaresoftware.html.

[118] WALTER, C. D. Improved linear systolic array for fast modular exponentiation. *IEE Proceedings Computers & Digital Techniques 147*, 5 (2000), 323–328.

[119] WANNEMACHER, M. *Das FPGA-Kochbuch*. MITP-Verlag, 1998.

[120] WU, M., ZENG, X., HAN, J., WU, Y., AND FAN, Y. A High-Performance Platform-Based SoC for Information Security. In *Conference on Asia South Pacific design automation (ASP-DAC)* (New York, NY, USA, 2006), ACM Press, pp. 122–123.

[121] XILINX. Platform Studio and the EDK. http://www.xilinx.com/ise/embedded_design_prod/platform_studio.htm.

[122] XILINX. Xilinx XUP Virtex-II Pro Development System. http://www.xilinx.com/univ/xupv2p.html.

[123] XILINX. *Virtex-II Pro and Virtex-II Pro X Platform FPGAs: Complete Data Sheets*, June 2005. http://www.xilinx.com/products/.

Die VDM Verlagsservicegesellschaft sucht für wissenschaftliche Verlage abgeschlossene und herausragende

Dissertationen, Habilitationen, Diplomarbeiten, Master Theses, Magisterarbeiten usw.

für die kostenlose Publikation als Fachbuch.

Sie verfügen über eine Arbeit, die hohen inhaltlichen und formalen Ansprüchen genügt, und haben Interesse an einer honorarvergüteten Publikation?

Dann senden Sie bitte erste Informationen über sich und Ihre Arbeit per Email an *info@vdm-vsg.de*.

Sie erhalten kurzfristig unser Feedback!

VDM Verlagsservicegesellschaft mbH
Dudweiler Landstr. 99   Telefon +49 681 3720 174
D - 66123 Saarbrücken   Fax   +49 681 3720 1749
www.vdm-vsg.de

Die VDM Verlagsservicegesellschaft mbH vertritt

Printed by Books on Demand GmbH, Norderstedt / Germany